TABLE OF CONTENTS

FIGURES

TABLES

PREFACE

This report is a contribution to the ongoing debate about whether the authorizations in Title 10 of the U.S. Code for general and flag officers (G/FOs) specify appropriate numbers and pay grades. Congress has not revised G/FO authorizations since 1996. The report addresses, in particular, the issues of whether the numbers and/or pay grades of G/FOs in the reserve component (RC) are commensurate with the increasing reliance upon the reserve forces in military operations, and whether G/FO strength in the RC is equitable compared to G/FO strength in the active component (AC). The report sheds light on these questions by examining current Title 10 authorizations and their near-term background and by providing a longer-term historical account of the fluctuations in G/FO levels in the AC over the entire post–World War II period.

The report proposes that the salient concerns when G/FO levels are considered for the AC and the RC, respectively, have always differed. In the AC, the preoccupation tends to be with the size of the G/FO corps. Appropriate size is viewed as a function in part of the overall size of the force, and is often measured as a troop-to-officer ratio or proportion. In the RC, the preoccupation is with the degrees of institutional power that the RC's top officers can wield within the Pentagon and other decision-making venues. This preoccupation with greater institutional power or "voice" has mainly translated over the years into campaigns to increase the authorizations and opportunities for reserve G/FOs to serve above the two-star level, rather than campaigns to increase the overall size of the reserve G/FO corps. This different preoccupation—i.e., with G/FO pay grades rather than numbers—in turn has meant that discussions about reserve G/FO strength are carried on without any systematic or longitudinal reference to troop-to-officer ratios or other such measures of proportional officer strength. Such measures of proportional numerical strength would be less meaningful in connection with the RC, because the claims that greater reserve G/FO strength are warranted do not rest on how large the reserve force is, but on how intensively it is used. Moreover, measures of proportional numerical strength would be, in any case, very challenging to use with reference to the RC, because of the plethora of categories of reservists, the shifts of duty status that reservists experience, and other factors.

KEY FINDINGS

- Title 10 of the U.S. Code currently specifies a basic number ceiling of 877 for general and flag officers (G/FOs) in the active component (AC). This number has remained unchanged since 1996, when Congress allocated 12 additional billets to the Marine Corps. In addition, since 1996, Title 10 has allowed for a pool of 12 positions—the Chairman's 12—that the services can use to fill joint-duty positions that do not count against the services' basic ceilings.

- Seen in an historical perspective, the AC's current total Title 10 allowance of 889 G/FO positions represents a low number in absolute terms. Prior to the end of the Cold War and since World War II, AC G/FO authorizations in Title 10 have always exceeded 1,000, often by some 100s.

- Although low in absolute terms, current AC G/FO authorizations are high in proportional terms, that is, high in proportion to the total size of the AC force or in proportion to enlisted personnel. During the post–Cold War drawdown, the AC enlisted force was reduced by about a third, a somewhat more drastic reduction than the reduction affecting officers, including G/FOs.

- The intention of Congress at the beginning of the 1990s drawdown of the AC was to maintain the then prevailing enlisted-to-officer (E–O) ratio, that classic measure of how officer-heavy a military force is. However, the 1990s saw a decline in this ratio from about 6:1 to about 5:1 enlisted-to-officer personnel.

- During the 1990s drawdown, the G/FO corps fared particularly well, in that the proportion of its actual reduction was even less than that of other officers. Although changes in G/FO numbers during the drawdown varied by service, there was a general shift toward an older, higher-ranking officer corps.

- Trends seen in the 1990s AC drawdown, such as the proportional increase in G/FOs and the decline in the E–O ratio, were in line with longer-term trends in the U.S. military. Although the military has exhibited a pattern of build-up and drawdown since World War II, and the size of the officer corps fluctuates along with fluctuations in overall force size, the overall trend has been for the E–O ratio to decline and for the average grade of the force to rise.

- Some critics of this trend complain of the "top-sizing" of the military, and criticize the tendency of the Department of Defense (DOD) to identify more requirements for officers, including G/FOs, than Congress is willing to authorize. Critics charge that the DOD, when reducing the force, finds it easier to reduce enlisted personnel and tends to protect officers and officer billets.

- Others say the trends that yield lower E–O ratios in the AC are justified by changed societal and military realities. Broad, general explanations for the declining E–O ratio specify at least two causes, the long-term decline of labor-intensive functions in the military relative to technologically skilled functions, and the increased demand for managerial skill, given the military's greater organizational complexity over time.

- Apart from such general and long-term causes for the growing proportion of officers, the more proximate cause most often cited is the growth in the demands the joint community levies upon the services to provide officers to fill joint-duty positions.

- The demand for AC officers, as some point out, has also grown with increasing use of the reserves, because reserve units sometimes have AC commanders.

- In connection with the reserves, the Congressional concern with G/FO numbers/grades has been slower to develop than the concern with the AC's numbers. Title 10 now specifies a basic number ceiling of 422 G/FOs for the RC. In addition, the RC is allowed some 178 G/FO slots for state and territorial adjutants general and their assistants, for officers at the National Guard Bureau, and for certain reserve officers whose status has shifted to active duty.

- Once introduced into national legislation, the number ceilings for RC G/FOs did not change. The first mention of such a number ceiling for the RC occurred in 1958, when the Army Reserve ceiling of 207 was specified. Other current service-specific reserve G/FO ceilings were established with the passage in 1994 of the Defense Authorization Act for Fiscal Year 1995.

- Congressionally mandated DOD studies of G/FO requirements have appeared over the years—in 1966, 1972, 1978, 1988, 1997, and 2003—but the first fully to integrate both the AC and RC requirements was the study mandated for 1997.

- While RC G/FO number authorizations, once established, remained the same, the overall size of the RC force, like that of the AC, has been subject to expansions and contractions, including the major 1990s contraction. In the 1990s drawdown, both RC enlisted and officer numbers were cut, albeit less severely than AC numbers.

- The 1990s drawdown of the RC and other fluctuations of RC numbers since World War II have not prompted analysts of the RC to calculate and track E–O ratios or other such measures. The calculation and longitudinal tracking of E–O ratios, common practices used to assess the "officer-heaviness" of the AC, rarely, if ever, figure in analyses of the RC.

- Such practices would yield less meaningful results in connection with the RC for a variety of reasons. For one thing, E–O ratios and other such measures are problematic to calculate for the RC, because of the variety of categories of reservists and because of their shifts of status as they move to and from active duty. More importantly, the assessment of whether the RC has appropriate G/FO strength has not focused primarily on the numerical strength of either the reserve force or the G/FO corps, but on the intensity of the reserve force's use by the military.

- For reserve advocates, the more intensive use of the reserves in recent years, rather than the RC's size, warrants greater reserve G/FO strength. However, G/FO strength is not seen primarily as numerical strength, but as sufficient representation in the military's highest ranks. Such advocates have focused their energies largely on upgrading the RC's top leadership, pressing for authorizations that allow the top reserve officers to hold positions above O–8.

- Along with seeking more authorizations for higher-ranked billets, reserve advocates have sought to ensure reserve officers access to the experience—mostly joint-duty experience—that is a prerequisite for promotion to higher office. They have campaigned for, and recently succeeded in gaining, Title 10 guarantees that a certain number of joint-duty positions will be held by one- and two-star reserve G/FOs.

INTRODUCTION

The dramatic increase in the use of the reserve forces since the end of the Cold War and, especially, since 9/11 has lent urgency to questions concerning the appropriate numbers and pay grades of reserve officers, including general and flag officers (G/FOs). For almost two decades, advocates for the reserve components have argued that reserve G/FO strength is not commensurate with the increased reliance on the reserve forces in military operations. During the 1990s, however, these advocates faced a challenging situation in which to press for different G/FO authorizations in Title 10 of the U.S. Code, because the military as a whole experienced a major congressionally mandated post–Cold War drawdown, including a reduction in officer strength at all ranks. The Department of Defense (DOD) reduced its military and civilian personnel by almost a third, and the officer corps fell to its smallest size since 1950.[1]

With G/FO positions a scarcer resource than during the Cold War, the military services' active components have had heightened incentives to resist any increased reserve G/FO authorizations that threatened to be at the expense of officers in the active components. At the same time, the reserve components, in view of their increased use, have had ever more reason to consider themselves shortchanged in senior officer strength compared to the active components.

Adjudicating the current concern, even competition, between the active and reserve force in regard to G/FOs requires understanding the major preoccupations over time of the active and reserve components, respectively, in regard to their officer corps, and appreciating the ways in which the military's active and reserve components have asserted the need for changes in the numbers and/or pay grades of their G/FOs. Discussions of the appropriate levels of G/FOs in the active and reserve components, respectively, center on quite different concerns, and the arguments offered for change run along considerably different lines. Active component (AC) concerns center and have centered on the overall size of the G/FO corps—i.e., the issue of the

---

[1] Harry J. Thie and Jefferson P. Marquis, *The Present Military Personnel Management Framework: Where It Came From*, PM–1247–OSD, September 2001, 6, http://www.defenselink.mil/prhome/docs/military_hr_stratplan3.pdf.

adequacy of numbers—while reserve component (RC) concerns have centered primarily on the grades of specific billets of the top leadership and on opportunities for officers to acquire qualifications, especially joint-duty experience, for promotion to higher grades.

In both the AC and RC components, a rough linkage exists between the overall size of the force and the number of officers at various ranks. Legislation presumes and reinforces this linkage. However, it is only in connection with the active components that systematic reference to this troop-officer relationship figures in debates about appropriate G/FO authorizations. In connection with the active components, it has been a common practice of personnel analysts and policymakers to highlight this troop-officer or force-size-to-officer relationship and to track its fluctuations over time. Often such longitudinal tracking has entailed the use of enlisted-to-officer (E–O) ratios, a classic measure of how officer-heavy a military force is.

In connection with the active components, references to falling enlisted-to-officer ratios over time have been used by opponents of increased officer authorizations to support their position. Such opponents criticize the services, for example, for failing to maintain, as they were charged to do, their fiscal year (FY) 1990 enlisted-to-officer ratios during the 1990s drawdown. Instead, as such critics point out, the 1990s saw the continuation of the long-term post–World War II trend in which the proportion of officers to enlisted personnel in the AC rose somewhat, with the proportion of G/FOs rising disproportionately.

Proponents of a larger AC G/FO corps, like opponents, refer to the enlisted-to-officer ratio and acknowledge its falling trend. However, they do so to justify the decline. Typically, they marshal reasons why the ratios of the past are less pertinent than previously and enumerate new conditions that explain lower E–O ratios. In the 1990s, the main new condition cited as necessitating more officers has been the demand for officers to fill an ever-growing number of joint-duty positions—positions above and beyond those required by the individual services.

In connection with the reserves, by contrast with the AC, references to E–O ratios rarely figure in discussions about the appropriate G/FO authorizations for the reserves. For a variety of reasons, the line of argument about ratios—a classic way to gauge appropriate officer authorizations—is not particularly effective. Neither opponents nor proponents of changes in reserve G/FO authorizations make the effort to use longitudinal data to work out with any precision the reserve enlisted-to-officer ratio.

Ratios are not effective in part because of the statistical challenges that the reserves pose. The diversity of the reserves precludes representing the proportion of reserve officers to their troops in a single, longitudinally trackable ratio. Within the military's seven reserve components, there are numerous reserve categories of service, each with subcategories.[2] This plethora of types of service for both officers and enlisted personnel means that the enlisted-to-officer ratio could be figured in numerous ways.

Another complication mitigating against the use of E–O ratios is that the status of a reservist shifts under particular conditions of service. Most reservists are normally classified as "in an active status" and appear on the Reserve Active Status List. However, after a period of time on active duty—until 2004, usually 180 days—their status becomes that of a soldier on the Active Duty List.[3] Although years of debate culminated in 2004 in lengthening the time period, the problem for counting purposes remains. Shifts of duty status complicate straightforward measures of appropriate officer levels, such as E–O ratios.

Further complications with citing and tracking enlisted-to-officer ratios in connection with the reserves include the fact that active component officers have often been assigned to lead reserve units and that some reserve officers, namely, those in the National Guard, oversee troops whose roles can shift from federal to state duty. In short, a number of factors mean that sheer force size bears a much less meaningful relationship to officer corps size in the RC than in the AC.

Although the challenges of establishing the enlisted-to-officer ratio or similar measures for the reserve components mitigate against their use, the unavailability of such measures hardly matters in discussions of reserve G/FO authorizations, because the discussions have not in any case centered on the sheer numbers of reserve G/FOs that would be desirable. Advocates for the reserves, in seeking to establish that the reserve components have been shortchanged in G/FO strength, have not primarily attempted to make the case that the overall size of the reserve G/FO corps has been too small or out of line with what would be warranted by troop numbers.[4] Rather,

---

[2] On the categories of reservists, see Appendix 2, below. See also the DOD study on which the Appendix is based: U.S. Department of Defense, Office of the Assistant Secretary of Defense (Reserve Affairs), *Reserve Component Categories of the Reserve Components of the Armed Forces* (Rev. September 2005), http://www.defenselink.mil/ra/documents/RC101%20Handbook-updated%2020%20Sep%2005.pdf.

[3] William Cohen, "Report of the Chairman of the Reserve Forces Policy Board," in *Annual Report to the President and the Congress*, 2000, http://www.dod.mil/execsec/adr2000/index.html.

[4] If an attempt were made to show that reserve G/FO number ceilings are smaller than warranted, given the size of the reserve force, the attempt would likely be frustrated by the fact that Title 10 reserve G/FO authorizations, once

the advocates have focused on the fact that the reserve components have lacked sufficient opportunities for promotion above O–8. The concern about the dearth of opportunities for reservists above O–8 has manifested itself in two efforts. One has been the effort to ensure that at least the top leadership of the reserve components should be assured appointment to a rank above the two-star level. The second effort has been to ensure the availability to reserve officers of opportunities to gain the joint-duty qualifications that are the prerequisite for appointment to the highest military ranks. Both efforts manifest the primary preoccupation of the RC with respect to G/FOs, the preoccupation with upgrading certain top officers, rather than with increasing the size of the overall general officer pool. The chief arguments in favor of increased reserve officer representation above O–8 have referred to the need for the reserves to have a stronger voice in decision-making venues in the military.

The contrast between the AC and the RC in their approaches to defining the issue of appropriate G/FO strength has been manifest for several decades in exchanges between the Department of Defense and Congress about officer requirements and authorizations. Such exchanges are a perennial feature of the U.S budget process and have culminated over the years in the authorizations for G/FOs passed by Congress and specified in Title 10 of the U.S. Code. The contrasting preoccupations of the AC and the RC can be seen reflected in these G/FO authorizations, as well as in the debates that lead to them. The preoccupations can be seen particularly in the modifications—often slight—that are periodically introduced, such as recently introduced exemptions from Title 10 G/FO number ceilings. In order to advance the understanding of the concerns of the AC and RC in current and future policy debates about G/FOs, this report offers, first, a description and discussion of current Title 10 authorizations and their immediate background and, second, a longer-perspective historical account of past authorizations for both the AC and the RC.

CURRENT LEGISLATIVE LIMITS ON G/FO NUMBERS AND PAY GRADES

Questions of equity between the active and reserve components come under the purview of Congress, because Congress is the final arbiter of resources for the military. In its role as final

---

specified, have not changed, while the size of the force has fallen over the course of the 1990s. The size of the force has not fallen by as large a percentage as has the AC force, but in the AC, the numbers of G/FOs and G/FO authorizations also fell. For numbers that can be compared, see Appendix 1, below.

arbiter, Congress has much to say about G/FOs as it enacts yearly defense authorizations and, eventually, rolls changes into Title 10 of the U.S. Code. In addressing the general officer population, Title 10 covers the four military services—the Army, the Air Force, the Navy, and the Marine Corps—and the four ranks that Congress has established above the rank of colonel or, for the Navy, captain. General officers of the Army, Air Force, or Marine Corps and flag officers of the Navy include O–7 (i.e., brigadier general, rear admiral [lower half]), O–8 (i.e., major general, rear admiral), O–9 (i.e., lieutenant general, vice admiral), and O–10 (i.e., general, admiral).[5] Table 1 displays the pay grade designation, title of rank, and insignia worn by officers at general and flag officer ranks.[6]

Table 1. Pay Grade, Title, and Insignia Worn at General and Flag Officer Ranks

Pay grade	Army, Air Force, Marine Corps	Navy	Insignia
O–10	General	Admiral	4 stars
O–9	Lieutenant general	Vice admiral	3 stars
O–8	Major general	Rear admiral	2 stars
O–7	Brigadier general	Rear admiral (lower half)	1 star

Source: Based on Title 10 U.S. Code and U.S. Government Accountability Office (GAO), *Military Personnel: DOD Could Make Greater Use of Existing Legislative Authority to Manage General and Flag Officer Careers*, GAO–04–1003, Washington, DC, September 2004, 11, http://www.gao.gov/cgi-bin/getrpt?GAO-04-1003.

In considering the officer corps at these ranks, Title 10 covers both the active and reserve components of the armed forces. The reserve forces comprise six components: Army National Guard, Army Reserve, Navy Reserve, Marine Corps Reserve, Air National Guard, and Air Force Reserve. A seventh reserve component, the Coast Guard Reserve, and its parent service fall under the Department of Homeland Security.

Among the issues of concern to Congress, as reflected in Title 10 in regard to the AC and RC, respectively, are the overall size of the G/FO corps, the service-specific G/FO end strengths, and the officer pay-grade balance. Title 10 governs the size and composition of the general

[5] The Coast Guard, which includes the Coast Guard Reserve (USCGR), is not under the Department of Defense and is not covered in Title 10. Laws applicable to the Coast Guard Reserve are set forth in chapter 21 of Title 14 (14 U.S.C. 701 et seq.). Although certain authorizations come from defense quarters, USCGR appropriations come from the transportation committees.
[6] The number of pay grades in the force has been reasonably stable: 10 commissioned officer, five warrant officer, nine enlisted. E–8 and E–9 and O–9 and O–10 were added in 1958, and W–5 was added in 1993. O–11 was used

officer population by prescribing both number and pay-grade ceilings. The ceilings are designed to ensure against officer strength overages and officer pay-grade imbalances. The G/FO authorizations are currently set forth mainly in Title 10's sections 525 and 526 for the active components and section 12004 for the reserve components. In addition to establishing end-strength limits and pay-grade distribution ceilings, Title 10 specifies the rank that certain positions hold—positions often carrying the requirement that appointment be with the advice and consent of the Senate. In the active components, such statutorily designated positions include the service chiefs of staff, the chairman and vice chairman of the Joint Chiefs of Staff, and the combatant commanders—all designated as O–10. In the reserve components, the statutorily designated positions include the chief of the National Guard Bureau—slated as of 2007 to be a four-star position—and, since the passage of Pub.L.No. 106–65, National Defense Authorization Act for Fiscal Year 2000, the reserve service chiefs of staff and the directors of the Army and the Air Force National Guard—all now three-star positions.[7] The reserve component chiefs hold the top offices in the commands specified in Title 10, sections 3038 (Army Reserve), 5143 (Navy Reserve), 5144 Marine Forces Reserve), and 8038 (Air Force Reserve).

In the case of the reserve forces, the application of Title 10 ceilings presents certain complications not encountered in the active components. One complication is that the status of a reservist is subject to shifts to that of an active-duty soldier. That is, for promotion, accounting, and other purposes, a reservist on active duty can shift to the Active Duty List (ADL) from, usually, the Reserve Active Status List (RASL).[8] When such a shift occurs, the reservist counts against active component ceilings rather than reserve ceilings. Another complication is that, in each of the services, a number of categories of reserves exists—a ready reserve, a standby

---

through September 1980. See Thie and Marquis, 6, http://www.defenselink.mil/prhome/docs/military_hr_stratplan3.pdf.

[7] Pub.L.No. 106–65, *National Defense Authorization Act for Fiscal Year 2000*, 113 Stat 512, October 5, 1999.

[8] For definitions of the two lists, see U.S. Department of Defense, *DOD Instruction, Number 1332.32*, December 27, 2006, http://www.dtic.mil/whs/directives/corres/pdf/133232p.pdf. The DOD Instruction, which refers to pertinent sections in Title 10, contains the following definitions:

> E1.1. Active Duty List. A single list for the Army, the Navy, the Air Force, or the Marine Corps required to be maintained under section 620 of Reference (d) that contains the names of all officers of that Military Service other than officers described in section 641 of Reference (d) who are serving on active duty.
>
> E1.4. Reserve Active Status List. A single list for the Army, the Navy, the Air Force, or the Marine Corps, required to be maintained under section 14002 of Reference (d), that contains the names of all officers of that Armed Force, except warrant officers (including commissioned

reserve, and a retired reserve—not all of which are included in end-strength counts for the purposes of Title 10 limitations. Title 10 number ceilings apply to a subset of all reservists, albeit a subset consisting of the great majority of reservists. The subset, in the wording of Title 10, comprises officers "in an active status." This category includes almost all officers in the Ready Reserve, with its two major subcategories of Selected Reserve and Individual Ready Reserve, but excludes officers in the Standby Reserve, the Retired Reserve, and the very small pool of Ready Reservists within the Army National Guard, namely, the Inactive National Guard.[9] Officers "in an active status" are actively involved in a reserve program or activities, e.g., training at a certain level, or even in operations, and appear on the RASL. Such reserve officers, even when ordered to active duty or in a full-time military job, do not exchange their status—i.e., active status—for that of personnel on the ADL in the active components, except after a specific period of time or under particular conditions. Until that shift of status occurs—traditionally after 180 days but after a longer period since 2004—the reserve officer counts against reserve end strength ceilings.[10] Thereafter, the officer counts against AC ceilings or, in the words of Title 10, section 12004, becomes someone "counted under section 526 of this title."

---

warrant officers) who are in an active status in a Reserve component of the Army, the Navy, the Air Force, or the Marine Corps and are not on an Active Duty List.

[9] Included in the Ready Reserve, the Selected Reserve provides trained and ready units and individuals to augment the active forces during times of war or national emergency, while the Individual Ready Reserve is a manpower pool that can be called to active duty during times of war or national emergency and would normally be used as individual fillers for active, guard and reserve units, and as a source of combat replacements. By contrast with the Ready Reserve, the Standby Reserve and Retired Reserve are not in an active status. The Standby Reserve cannot be called to active duty, other then for training, unless authorized by Congress under "full mobilization." The Retired Reserve represents an even lower potential for involuntary mobilization. On these categories, see Appendix 2.

[10] See Albert C. Zapanta, "Transforming Reserve Forces," *Joint Force Quarterly*, December 2004, 4, http://www.defenselink.mil/releases/release.aspx?releaseid=2742. Enacted in October 2004, the National Defense Authorization Act for Fiscal Year 2005 (Pub.L.No. 108–375, 118 Stat 1811, October 28, 2004) eliminated the 180-day rule. According to new rules, reserve forces officers who are called to active duty, with their consent, for three years or less, are retained on the RASL, rather than being placed on the ADL. Previously, only officers voluntarily serving on active duty for 180 days or less were exempt from being placed on the ADL. Reserve component officers on active duty for up to three years can now be considered for promotion by a reserve promotion selection board rather than an active-duty promotion selection board. The point at which at which reserve G/FOs on active duty should begin to be included in active end strength counts has not just been subject to variation over time. The timing of the shift of status has also been a function of a reservist's type of service. For example, a reservist serving on voluntary active duty orders may shift after a shorter interval than a reservist serving in support of combatant commands.

Current General/Flag Officer Authorizations: Number Ceilings

In prescribing the DOD-wide ceilings for G/FOs for both the active and reserve components, Title 10 gives the basic total of senior officers that each component is not to exceed, plus certain exemptions that do not count against the authorized officer end strength for that component. As described below, these exemptions from end strength counts mainly involve, in the active components, joint-duty positions and, in the reserve components, positions that entail responsibilities prescribed under Title 32 of the U.S. Code.

The current basic authorization for active-duty G/FOs, minus exemptions, is 877 (10 U.S.C. 526(a)). This number was first established when the National Defense Authorization Act for Fiscal Year 1997 slightly raised the DOD-wide ceiling by incorporating the 1996 authorization of 12 additional G/FO positions for the Marine Corps.[11] The current authorization for reserve component G/FOs is 422.

Active and Reserve Component Service-Specific Number Ceilings

Title 10 promulgates not only the G/FO number ceiling for each component, but also the share of that total allotted to each service. The number of general officers on active duty in the Army, Air Force, and Marine Corps, and the number of flag officers on active duty in the Navy, may not exceed the number specified for the armed force concerned, as stipulated in Title 10, section 526.[12] Title 10, section 12004, "Strength in Grade: Reserve General and Flag Officers in an Active Status," authorizes the service-specific G/FO numbers for the reserve components. Current Title 10 numbers for both components are shown in Table 2.

---

[11] Congress authorized the 12 new positions as part of Pub.L.No. 104–201, *National Defense Authorization Act for Fiscal Year 1997*, section 405, 110 Stat 2422, 2506, September 23, 1996. See also U.S. General Accounting Office (GAO), *General And Flag Officers: DOD's Study Needs Adjustments: Testimony Before the Subcommittee on Military Personnel, Committee on National Security, House of Representatives* (statement of Mark E. Gebicke, Director, Military Operations and Capabilities Issues, National Security and International Affairs Division), GAO/T–NSIAD–97–122, April 8, 1997, 3, http://www.gao.gov/archive/1997/ns97122t.pdf.

[12] 10 U.S.C. 526, http://www.oscn.net/applications/oscn/DeliverDocument.asp?CiteID=192504.

Table 2. Current Authorized End Strengths of G/FOs

Service	Active Component	Reserve Component
Army	302	207
Air Force	279	157
Navy	216	48
Marine Corps	80	10
Total	**877**	**422**
Source: Based on Title 10, sections 526 and 12004.		

In the specifications of the numbers for the reserves, Title 10 does not detail how the Army and the Air Force numbers are to be divided between each service's two reserve components, their Reserve and National Guard components.

Chairman's 12: Exemptions From the Active G/FO Number Ceiling

Although the DOD-wide ceiling for AC general and flag officers has been set at 877 since fiscal year 1997, Congress has in actuality authorized a somewhat higher number. Title 10, section 526(b), provides up to an additional 12 general officer billets above and beyond the individual service authorizations, specifying that the positions must be used by the services to fill the requirements for joint duty levied upon the services by the joint community. Commonly referred to as the "Chairman's 12," these 12 G/FO positions were originally scheduled to remain available only until expiration in October 1998.[13] However, they have been repeatedly reauthorized. Still in effect, the Chairman's 12 are not statutorily associated with specific positions. As provided in 10 USC 526(b), the chairman of the Joint Chiefs of Staff designates and controls the positions, allocating them to the services. Only the Marine Corps receives no such allocations, because of its small pool of G/FOs at the O–9 and O–10 levels.[14] The addition

---

[13] U.S. General Accounting Office (GAO), *General And Flag Officers: DOD's Study Needs Adjustments: Testimony Before the Subcommittee on Military Personnel, Committee on National Security, House of Representatives*, NSIAD–97–122, April 8, 1997, 6, http://www.gao.gov/archive/1997/ns97122t.pdf.

[14] U.S. Government Accountability Office (GAO), *Military Personnel: General and Flag Officer Requirements Are Unclear Based on DOD's 2003 Report to Congress*, GAO–04–488, April 2004, 9. Generally speaking, the Marines have a low percentage of G/FOs, and their share is disproportionately low in relation to force size when compared to the other services. In 2000, for example, the actual Marine Corps share of G/FOs was 9 percent, while the Army had 36 percent, the Air Force had 30 percent, and the Navy had 25 percent. See Thie and Marquis, 8.

of the Chairman's 12 positions to the 877 G/FOs currently authorized for the services results in a total authorization of 889 G/FOs in the active components.[15]

Table 3 summarizes the current Title 10 authorizations for the active and reserve components, including the "Chairman's 12."

Table 3. Congressional Authorizations for G/FOs by Service and Component

Service	**Active Component**			**Reserve Component**	
	Service Ceiling	**Chairman's 12**		**Reserve component**	**Total**
Army	302	5		207	**514**
Air Force	279	3		157	**439**
Navy	216	4		48	**268**
Marine Corps	80	0		10	**90**
Total	**877**	**12**		**422**	**1,311**

Sources: Based on Title 10 U.S. Code and U.S. Government Accountability Office (GAO), *Military Personnel: General and Flag Officer Requirements Are Unclear Based on DOD's 2003 Report to Congress*, GAO–04–488, Washington, DC, April 2004, http://www.gao.gov/cgi-bin/getrpt?GAO-04-488.

Exemptions From the Reserve G/FO Number Ceiling

Like the active components, with their Chairman's 12 allowances, the reserve components have been given G/FO ceiling exemptions that provide end-strength relief. However, the major form of number ceiling relief for the reserves differs from that of the active components. Unlike the Chairman's 12, which offers end-strength relief for joint duty, the relief for the reserves mainly compensates for the state responsibilities of the National Guard. In recognition of the fact that Guard officers fulfill state—i.e., Title 32—responsibilities, as well as federal DOD responsibilities, Congress has exempted from the Title 10 reserve officer ceiling a number of reserve G/FOs serving in specific positions that carry Title 32 responsibilities. As stipulated in Title 10, section 12004(b), the general officers not counted for purposes of the service-specific ceilings in the reserves include the following three categories:

- Those serving as adjutants general or assistant adjutants general of a state

- Those serving in the National Guard Bureau—Army and Air Force Guard officers

---

[15]See U.S. Department of Defense, Chairman of the Joint Chiefs of Staff, "Manpower And Personnel Actions Involving General and Flag Officers," *Chairman of the Joint Chiefs of Staff Instruction (CJCSI) 1331.01C*, July 22, 2005, current as of July 31, 2006, http://www.dtic.mil/cjcs_directives/cdata/unlimit/1331_01.pdf.

- Those counted under section 526 of this title, i.e., those whose status has shifted from "active status" to active duty.

The three categories of exemptions provided by section 12004(b) add up to significant numbers beyond the basic Title 10 ceiling of 422, given that all 54 states and territories have adjutants general and assistant adjutants general. When reviewed in March 1997, for example, the exemptions allowed for an additional 178 general officers in the reserve components above and beyond the then already established limit of 422.[16]

While the exemptions promulgated in Title 10, section 12004, do not provide the RC with G/FO end-strength relief to use for joint-duty billets, Title 10 is not silent on the question of joint-duty billets for reserve G/FOs. Title 10, section 526, provides for 11 joint-duty billets to be specifically designated for officers in the reserve components. The positions include the so-called "Chairman's 10," which was first established by the Fiscal Year 2000 National Defense Authorization Act, plus one position added in 2006.[17] As described in 10 USC 526(b)(2)(A), the reserve-designated positions are either O–7 or O–8 in the unified combatant commands. One example of such a set-aside position is the two-star chief of staff position in USNORTHCOM's headquarters.

The reserve-designated joint-duty positions—the Chairman's 10 plus one—are not fully analogous to the Chairman's 12 and other special exemptions for the active components, in that the reserve positions were designed as joint-duty set-asides rather than end-strength relief. The O–7 and O–8 set-aside positions do not count against the number ceilings for active-component G/FOs. Thus, the positions augment the opportunities for RC officers to gain joint-duty credentials, without being at the expense of the active-component G/FO numbers.[18]

---

[16] U.S. General Accounting Office (GAO), *General and Flag Officers: Number Required is Unclear Based on DOD's Draft Report*, GAO/NSIAD–97–160, Washington, DC, June 1997, 7, http://www.gao.gov/archive/1997/ns97160.pdf.

[17] For the law that amended Title 10 to establish the "Chairman's 10," see Pub.L.No.106–65, *National Defense Authorization Act for Fiscal Year 2000*, 113 Stat 512, October 5, 1999. For the law that amended Title 10 to establish the later additional joint position, see Pub.L.No. 109–163, *National Defense Authorization Act for Fiscal Year 2006*, section 510, 119 Stat 3136, 3231, January 6, 2006.

[18] Commission on the National Guard and Reserves, Congressional Transcripts, Congressional Hearings, "Commission on the National Guard and Reserves Holds Hearing on National Guard and Reserve Operations and Roles," March 8, 2006, http://www.ngaus.org/ngaus/files/ccLibraryFiles/Filename/000000001265/Commission%20on%20Roles%20and%20Mission%203-8-06.pdf.

Reserve G/FOs on Extended Active Duty: A Complication for End Strength Counts

The precise number of G/FO positions that the AC and RC are allowed at any one time is subject to some variation, in large part because of the accounting complications posed by reserve G/FOs serving on extended active duty. Extended active-duty reservists are among those included in the third category of reserve ceiling exemptions mentioned in Title 10, section 12004, "those counted under section 526," i.e., those who count toward AC end strengths. Reserve officers serving on active duty cease after a certain lapse of time to count against reserve end-strength ceilings and begin to count against AC ceilings. The lapse of time has varied over time and depends on the reservist's type of service, e.g., service on voluntary active-duty orders or service in support of combatant commands.[19] Whether, and under what conditions, reserve G/FOs on active duty should cease to count against the reserve ceiling and begin to count instead against the AC ceiling has been a long-standing issue in discussions of G/FO authorizations in the U.S. military.[20] At issue in the discussions has been the amount of time that the reservists should serve in an active-duty billet before their status shifts and they count against the active component ceiling.

Until the enactment of the National Defense Authorization Act for Fiscal Year 2005, the "180-day rule" was in effect.[21] The rule had been established in 1980 when the Defense Officer Personnel Management Act (Pub.L.No. 96–513, §102) was enacted to amend Title 10 of the U.S. Code. According to the rule—in effect, accounting guidelines—RC service members who were mobilized for more than 179 days had to be counted against AC statistics (10 U.S.C. 526d). This provision changed, as a result of the National Defense Authorization Act for Fiscal Year 2005, to allow reservists to serve for longer periods before counting against AC end strengths and pay-grade limitations.[22] The rule change— expanding the time that reservists can retain Reserve Active Status—represented end-strength relief for the active components, because reservists

---

[19] Zapanta, 4.

[20] Reserve Officers Association, "ROA Legislative Initiatives," *The Officer*, May 2007, 18, http://www.roa.org/site/DocServer/0705_officer.pdf?docID=1961.

[21] U.S. Government Accountability Office (GAO), *Military Personnel: Reserve Components Need Guidance to Accurately and Consistently Account for Volunteers on Active Duty for Operational Support*, GAO–07–93, Washington, DC, October 2006, 2, http://www.gao.gov/new.items/d0793.pdf.

[22] "ROA Legislative Initiatives," 18.

could serve on extended active duty and still be excluded from counts of active G/FO end strengths.[23]

Current General/Flag Officer Grade Distribution (10 USC 525)

The legislative regulation of G/FO numbers addresses not only their end strengths in various parts of the total force, but also their distribution among the four pay grades above O–6. Title 10, along with setting number ceilings, establishes maximum, service-specific limits on the percentage that may serve in particular pay grades. In so doing, Title 10 covers the authorized distribution of G/FO pay grades more comprehensively for the active components than for the reserves. For the active components, Title 10 delineates the exact breakdown of the general officer force by grade authorizations. For the reserve components, whose officers have mainly been limited to O–7 and O–8, Title 10 explicitly addresses grade distribution only for some services.

Current Authorizations for Pay-Grade Distributions of Active Component G/FOs

Currently, pay-grade distribution in the active force is determined by the following requirements:

- No more than half of all general or flag officers in each service may serve in a pay grade above O–7.[24]

- No more than 15.7 percent of the general officers in the Army or Air Force or flag officers in the Navy may be appointed in a pay grade above major general or rear admiral (upper half). In the Marine Corps, no appointment may be made in a pay grade above major general if that appointment would result in more than 17.5 percent of the service's general officers on active duty being in pay grades above major general.[25]

- Of a service's general or flag officers in O–9 and O–10, no more than 25 percent may be in O–10.[26]

---

[23] Reservists also benefit in various ways from retaining their prior status, notwithstanding that the conversion of status would free up a G/FO billet for those officers who remain on the Reserve Active Status List. Reservists benefit from remaining on the Reserve Active Duty List in terms of opportunities for promotion, retirement benefits, and so on.
[24] 10 U.S.C., section 525(a).
[25] 10 U.S.C., section 525(b).
[26] This provision does not apply to the Marine Corps.

These current ceilings differ slightly from those of the late 1990s.[27] As of 2000, the O–9 and O–10 ceiling was raised to 15.7 percent from 15 percent for the Army, the Air Force, and the Navy.[28] As of 2002, the Marine Corps maximum for the same pay grades, already higher at 16.2 percent than the ceiling of the other services, was raised to 17.5.[29]

Table 4 shows the AC grade distribution as authorized by Title 10, as well as the relief provided by the Chairman's 12 exemptions.

Table 4. Authorized G/FO Distribution in Grade in the AC

	TOTAL	O–10	O–9	O–8	O–7	Remarks
Army	302	12	37	102	151	10 USC 526(a)
Air Force	279	10	34	95	140	
Navy	216	8	25	75	108	
Marine Corps	80	2	10	28	40	
SUBTOTAL	**877**	**32**	**106**	**300**	**439**	
10 USC 526(b)(1)						Chairman's 12
Army	307	12	36	105	154	5
Air Force	282	10	35	96	141	3
Navy	220	8	26	76	110	4
Marine Corps	80	2	10	28	40	0
TOTAL	**889**	**32**	**109**	**303**	**445**	12

Source: U.S. Department of Defense, Chairman of the Joint Chiefs of Staff, "Manpower And Personnel Actions Involving General and Flag Officers," *Chairman of the Joint Chiefs of Staff Instruction (CJCSI) 1331.01C*, July 22, 2005, current as of July 31, 2006, http://www.dtic.mil/cjcs_directives/cdata/unlimit/1331_01.pdf.

Table 5 below shows the actual percentage of officers competing for a promotion who were in fact promoted from O–7 to O–8 between 1998 and 2003, as well as the proportion who were considered for, and selected to enter, the G/FO pool initially. The actual percentage promoted to O–8 falls below the authorized maximum of 50 percent.

---

[27] U.S. Government Accountability Office (GAO), *Military Personnel: DOD Could Make Greater Use of Existing Legislative Authority to Manage General and Flag Officer Careers*, GAO–04–1003, Washington, DC, September 2004, 5, http://www.gao.gov/cgi-bin/getrpt?GAO-04-1003.

[28] For the law that amended Title 10 to change the grade ceiling for the Army, Air Force, and Navy, see Pub.L.No. 106–398, *National Defense Authorization Act for Fiscal Year 2001*, Appendix, section 507 (g)(1), 114 Stat 1654A–1, 1654A–105, October 30, 2000.

[29] For the law that amended Title 10 to change the grade ceiling for the Marine Corps, see Pub.L.No. 107–314, *National Defense Authorization Act for 2003*, Sec. 404(b), 116 Stat 2458, 2525, December 2, 2002.

Table 5. Actual Proportion of AC Officers Selected for Promotion to O–7 and O–8 Between Fiscal Years 1998 and 2003

Service	Promotion from O–6 to O–7			Promotion from O–7 to O–8		
	Number considered	Number selected	Percentage	Number considered	Number selected	Percentage
Army	10,120	240	2.4	395	186	47.1
Air Force	9,577	232	2.4	481	157	32.6
Navy	7,736	202	2.6	282	140	49.7
Marine Corps	1,679	58	3.4	66	47	71.2
Total	**29,112**	**732**	**2.5**	**1,224**	**530**	**43.3**

Source: Based on GAO analysis of military service data and U.S. Government Accountability Office (GAO), *Military Personnel: DOD Could Make Greater Use of Existing Legislative Authority to Manage General and Flag Officer Careers*, GAO–04–1003, Washington, DC, September 2004, 11, http://www. gao.gov/cgi-bin/get rpt?GAO-04-1003.

Active Component Exemptions From Pay-Grade Ceilings Above O–8

The pay-grade ceilings for each service, like the number ceilings, are not without some flexibility. Through a number of so-called "headspace" rules, Title 10 offers a number of exemptions from the AC grade ceilings. The exempt positions are drawn from the authorized O–8 population to allow for additional O–9 and O–10 slots within the total of 889 of AC general officers. These allowances, unlike the Chairman's 12, do not permit more officers overall, but permit a somewhat larger number to occupy top ranks, generally when serving on joint duty. Congress has provided the following pay-grade exemptions, by way of offering AC grade-limit relief:

(1) Three exemptions from the general/admiral ceiling for officers serving as the chairman and vice chairman of the Joint Chiefs of Staff and/or the chief of staff to the president (10 USC 525(b)(3)).

(2) Seven exemptions from the lieutenant general/vice admiral ceiling for officers in joint positions designated by the president (10 USC 525(b)(4)(B)).

(3) Eleven exemptions from the general/admiral grade ceiling for officers in certain senior joint positions such as a commander in chief of a unified or specified command. Originally authorized until September 30, 2000, the exemptions remain in force (10 USC 525((b)(5)(A).

(4) One exemption for a senior military assistant to the secretary of defense (10 USC 525(b)(8)).

(5) As stipulated in the Intelligence Reform and Terrorism Prevention Act of 2004 (section 103A(c)), one exemption for the director of national intelligence or principal deputy director of national intelligence, if the office-holder is an AC officer.

(6) When no officer is assigned to the positions of the director of central intelligence, deputy director of central intelligence, or deputy director of central intelligence for community management, one exemption for an officer assigned as the associate director of central intelligence for military support (10 USC 528).

(7) One exemption for the chief of the National Guard Bureau.

(8) Six exemptions for the Reserve chiefs of staff (Army, Air Force, Navy, and Marine Corps) and the Directors of the National Guard (Army and Air Force).

Table 6 below presents a summary of current authorizations for the active components, which shows that, apart from the Chairman's 12, various exemptions represent rank upgrades and do not add to the total officer pool. Such special exemptions allow the services to exceed the limits for the two pay grades above O–8, usually for the purpose of filling joint-duty billets and usually only while the appointed officer remains in the position.

Table 6. Available Distribution Of General/Flag Officers

	Total	O-10	O-9	O-8	O-7	REMARKS
Army	302	12	37	102	151	10 USC 526(a)
Air Force	279	10	34	95	140	
Navy	216	8	25	75	108	
Marine Corps	80	2	10	28	40	
Subtotal	**877**	**32**	**106**	**300**	**439**	
10 USC 526(b)(1)						Chairman's 12
Army	307	12	36	105	154	5
Air Force	282	10	35	96	141	3
Navy	220	8	26	76	110	4
Marine Corps	80	2	10	28	40	0
Subtotal	**889**	**32**	**109**	**303**	**445**	12
10 USC 525(b)(3)		2		-2		CJCS/VCJCS
Subtotal	**889**	**34**	**109**	**301**	**445**	
10 USC 525(b)(5)(A) and 604(b)			11	-11		Combatant CDR, USFK & DCDRUSEUCOM*
Subtotal	**889**	**34**	**120**	**290**	**445**	
10 USC 525(b)(4)(B)			7	-7		Joint Staff
Subtotal	**889**	**34**	**127**	**283**	**445**	
10 USC 525(b)(6)			1	-1		Chief, National Guard Bureau
Subtotal	**889**		**128**	**282**	**445**	
10 USC 528			1	-1		Assoc Dir of CIA for Military Support**
Subtotal	**889**	**36**	**127**	**281**	**445**	
10 USC 525(b)(8)	889		1	-1		SMA to the SecDef
Subtotal		**36**	**128**	**280**	**445**	
10 USC 525(b)(3)		1		-1		COS to President (Not Filled)
Subtotal	**889**	**37**	**128**	**279**	**445**	
10 USC 525(b)			3	-3		Sup, Service Academy's***
Subtotal	**889**	**37**	**131**	**276**	**445**	
Intel Reform Act '04		1		-1		Principal DepDir of Nat'l Intel
Subtotal	**889**	**38**	**131**	**275**	**445**	
10 USC 525(2)(b)(6), 3038, 5143, 5144, and 8038			6	-6		Reserve Chiefs/National Guard Directors
Total	**889**	**38**	**137**	**269**	**445**	
10 USC 526(a)					(10)	Chairman's 10****

*DEPCDRUSEUCOM only when the commander is also Supreme Allied Commander, Europe.
**Only when none of the positions identified in 10 USC 528 are officers of the armed forces.
***Only if the officer assigned agrees to retire upon termination from that assignment.
****10 Reserve G/FO authorizations count against Reserve end strength so not additive to active G/FO authorizations.

Source: U.S. Department of Defense, Chairman of the Joint Chiefs of Staff, "Manpower And Personnel Actions Involving General and Flag Officers," *Chairman of the Joint Chief of Staff Instruction (CJCSI) 1331.01C*, July 22, 2005, current as of July 31, 2006, http://www.dtic.mil/cjcs_directives/cdata/unlimit/ 1331_01.pdf.

The leeway provided by various exemptions in Title 10 yields actual G/FO numbers at specific grades that vary within a range. Moreover, authorizations are targets; there is always some over-manning or under-manning (which may be expressed as a percentage of authorizations, e.g., as 101 percent of authorizations). Table 7 below presents the actual distribution of AC general officer positions as of December 31, 2006, as well as the total manpower of each service at the time.[30]

Table 7. DOD Active-Duty Military Personnel by Rank/Grade

December 31, 2006

Rank/Grade - All	Army	Navy	Marine Corps	Air Force	Total Services
General – Admiral	12	10	6	12	40
Lt General – Vice Admiral	52	33	16	38	139
Maj General – Rear Admiral (U)	94	71	22	92	279
Brig General – Rear admiral (L)	150	110	39	144	443
Service Total	308	224	83	286	901
Total Active Manpower	502,466	345,566	178,477	345,024	1,371,533

Source: Based on U.S. Department of Defense, Defense Manpower Data Center, Statistical Information Analysis Division, "Armed Forces Strength Figures," http://siadapp.dior.whs.mil/ personnel/MILITARY/ms0.pdf.

Current Authorizations for Pay-Grade Distributions of Reserve Component G/FOs

Whereas Title 10 covers G/FO pay-grade distribution in the active components in some detail and for all the services, it does not specify the DOD-wide pay-grade mix for reserve G/FOs. That is, Title 10 does not state, as it does for the active components, what percentage of each service's total reserve G/FO pool may serve at a given rank. Title 10 offers some evidence of legislative intent that the pay-grade distribution below O–9 should parallel that of the active components. For instance, with respect to the Navy reserves, section 12004(c)(3) states: "Not more than 50 percent of the officers in an active status authorized under this section for the Navy may serve in the grade of rear admiral," meaning that half of the G/FOs are expected to serve in the lowest G/FO grade, as in the active forces. However, this rule is not explicitly stated for all the services, and there is no mention of percentages of G/FOs that should occupy higher ranks. The obvious reason is that virtually all reserve G/FOs hold one-star and two-star billets. Until 1979, when the chief of the National Guard (CNGB) billet was made a three-star position, no positions in the reserve components held a rank above O–8. It was not until 2000 that the reserves were authorized a number of other three-star billets, namely, six slots statutorily

---

[30] The Coast Guard figures, which total 40,829, are not included in the DOD total, because the Coast Guard reports to the Department of Homeland Security.

designated for the chiefs of the reserves and the directors of the National Guard.[31] In 2007 a long campaign by reserve advocates culminated in the agreement to authorize a fourth star for the CNGB. The addition of these authorizations for officer positions above O–8 still left the reserves with a relative dearth of such positions, making it pointless for Title 10 to specify pay-grade distribution percentages for O–9 and O–10 officers.

As with the Title 10 AC authorizations for G/FO grades and numbers, those for the RC yield a certain range in actual practice. In the case of the RC, the officers may be drawn from a number of categories of reservists, which means that determining the actual G/FO end strength at a given time may require adding the numbers from separate lists. In September 2005, the Defense Manpower Data Center reported the actual numbers of reservists by grade in two categories, Selected Reserve and Individual Ready Reserve/Inactive National Guard.[32] The numbers and grade distribution of G/FOs are shown in Table 8.

Table 8. Actual Numbers of G/FOs in the Reserves, 2005

Pay Grade	Selected Reserve	Individual Ready Reserve/ Inactive National Guard	Total
O–9	2	3	**5**
O–8	195	8	**203**
O–7	407	6	**413**
Total	**604**	**17**	**621**

Source: Based on U.S. Department of Defense, Defense Manpower Data Center, Statistical Information Analysis Division, *Selected Manpower Statistics*, "Table 5–15: Department of Defense, Total Distribution of the Individual Ready Reserve/Inactive National Guard by Grade," September 30, 2005, http://siadapp.dmdc.osd.mil/personnel/M01/fy05/m01fy05.pdf.

As Table 8 shows, the actual 2005 number of 621 somewhat exceeded the base Title 10 number of 422 plus exemptions, which added up to 600 in 1997.

---

[31] See the following Title 10 U.S.C. sections on the three-star ranks of the chiefs: 3038 for the Chief of the Army Reserve, 5143 for the Chief of the Navy Reserve, 5144 for the Marine Corps Commander, and 8038 for the Air Force.
[32] For a description of the Selected Reserve and its subcategories, see U. S. Department of Defense, Defense Manpower Data Center, *Description of Officers and Enlisted Personnel in the U.S. Selected Reserve, 1986, A Report Based on the 1986 Reserve Components Surveys,* n.d.

How Current G/FO Ceilings Relate to Other End-Strength Ceilings

The current size and grade composition of the G/FO corps, both authorized and actual and in both the AC and RC, bear systematic but somewhat loose relationships to the overall end strengths and grade mix of the two components, to the size of each component's enlisted force in each service, and to the size of the each component's officer corps in each service. Legislation presumes and reinforces these relationships, and sets forth ceilings accordingly for elements of the armed forces besides G/FOs. Annual defense authorizations, for example, set forth each year's end-strength limits for officers and enlisted personnel combined in, respectively, the AC and RC.[33] Current number ceilings for the active component as promulgated in the National Defense Authorization Act for Fiscal Year 2007 allow for a total force of nearly 1.37 million uniformed personnel, as shown in Table 9.[34]

Table 9. Authorized End Strengths for the Active Forces as of September 30, 2007

Service	
Army	512,400
Navy	340,700
Marine Corps	180,000
Air Force	334,200
DOD Total	1,367,300
Coast Guard	
Source: Based on *National Defense Authorization Act for Fiscal Year 2007*, Pub.L.No. 109–364, section 401, October 17, 2006, http://frwebgate.access. gpo.gov/cgi-bin/getdoc.cgi?dbname=109_cong_public_laws&docid=f:publ 364.109.pdf.	

The same legislation specifies ceilings for the main part of the Ready Reserve, namely, the Selected Reserve, the portion of the reserve force that is organized as units, as well as for a number of other, much smaller pools of reservists. Table 10 shows the ceilings for the Selected

---

[33] Title 10 also specifies certain ceilings for the reserve officer corps as a whole and for the reserve force as a whole, but the ceilings are maximums that greatly exceed the annual authorizations in the national defense authorization act. For example, Title 10, section 12003, specifies the following numbers for reserve commissioned officers (O–1 to O–10) in an active status: Army, 275,000; Air Force, 200,000; Navy, 150,000; and Marine Corps, 24,500. Title 10, section 12002, gives authorized maximums for the Army and Air Force reserve components, as follows: Army National Guard, 600,000; Army Reserve, 980,000, Air Force National Guard, 150,000, and Air Force Reserve, 500,000. Such numbers exceed recent authorizations by roughly three times.

[34] Pub.L.No. 109–364, *National Defense Authorization Act for Fiscal Year 2007*, 120 Stat 2083,October 17, 2006, http://frwebgate.access.gpo.gov/cgi-bin/getdoc.cgi?dbname=109_cong_public_laws&docid=f:publ364.109.pdf.

Reserve and for reservists on active duty for operational support. The latter do not count against the number ceilings for either the reserves or the active component.

Table 10. Authorized Strengths for Reserve Personnel As of September 30, 2007

Reserve Component	Selected Reserve	On Active Duty for Operational Support
Army National Guard (ARNG)	350,000	17,000
Army Reserve (USAR)	200,000	13,000
Navy Reserve (USNR)	71,300	6,200
Marine Corps Reserve (USMCR)	39,600	3,000
Air National Guard (ANG)	107,800	16,000
Air Force Reserve (USAFR)	74,900	14,000
DOD Total	**843,600**	**69,200**
Coast Guard Reserve (USCGR)	10,000	

Source: Based on *National Defense Authorization Act for Fiscal Year 2007*, section 401, http://fr webgate.access.gpo.gov/cgi-bin/getdoc.cgi?dbname=109_cong_public_laws& docid=f:publ364. 109.pdf.

The current authorized end strength of 843,600 for the Selected Reserve constitutes the largest but not the only significant part of reserve numbers "in an active status." Another large pool of reservists in an active status is the Individual Ready Reserve (IRR). Differing from the Selected Reserves, which provides units to augment active forces, the IRR is a pre-trained manpower pool that provides individuals to fill out active, Guard, and reserve units and to serve as casualty replacements. The IRR typically adds substantial numbers to reserve end strengths. For example, based on data reported by the Defense Manpower Data Center, the IRR, as of September 2005, numbered 284,421, including 237,425 enlisted personnel, 45,407 officers, and 1,409 warrant officers.[35] Adding the IRR numbers to those for the Selected Reserve from the same source yields a Ready Reserve total of about 1.089 million. Broken down by service, the IRR numbered 112,668 in the Army Reserve, 64,354 in the Navy Reserve, 59,882 in the Marine Corps Reserve, 41,319 in the Air Force Reserve, and 4,693 in the Coast Guard Reserve. The IRR total in 2005 was down somewhat, from about 312,000 in fiscal year 2002 and from about

---

[35] U.S. Department of Defense, Defense Manpower Data Center, Statistical Information Analysis Division, *Selected Manpower Statistics*, Table 5–15: Department of Defense, Total Distribution of the Individual Ready Reserve/Inactive National Guard by Grade - September 30, 2005, 172, http://siadapp.dmdc.osd.mil/personnel/M01/ fy05/m01fy05.pdf.

344,000 in fiscal year 2001.[36] The decrease in reported IRR figures for 2005 paralleled that in the Selected Reserve. The Selected Reserve, which totaled 811,147 in 2005, including 114,560 officers, was down from 874,000 in fiscal 2002 and from 867,000 in fiscal year 2001.[37]

As in the case of the active component, the requirement for officers—or, more particularly, G/FOs—in the reserve component is roughly linked to the size and mix of the forces they lead. The appropriate proportion of G/FOs and other officers in both the AC and RC, as determined by the Department of Defense's requirements process, depends on a number of major factors, many of which pertain to both active and reserve components, e.g. the number and types of force elements, such as divisions or air wings.[38] At the same time, the Title 10 authorizations for reserve G/FOs have been more stable than those for AC G/FOs. Once specified, reserve G/FO authorizations have remained unchanged, notwithstanding some fluctuations in the size and mix of the overall reserve force.[39]

Despite the general similarities of the G/FO requirements determination process in the AC and the RC, the issues of whether the proportion of the reserve G/FOs is appropriate, or the numbers equitable compared to the active component, cannot be resolved by simple comparisons with the active component. The different roles played by the AC and the RC affect their respective needs for officers. For example, because the AC uses the RC to augment active-duty forces, AC officers have often commanded RC units, adding to the AC officer end strengths the unit's service requires. Also affecting the efficacy of comparisons is the fact that the reserves

---

[36] *Population Representation in the Military Services Fiscal Year 2002*, March 2004, http://www.defenselink.mil/ prhome/poprep2002/pdf/intro2002.pdf; *Population Representation in the Military Services Fiscal Year 2001*, March 2003, http://www.defenselink.mil/prhome/poprep2001/pdf/Intro2001.pdf.

[37] *Population Representation in the Military Services Fiscal Year 2002*; *Population Representation in the Military Services Fiscal Year 2001*. The Defense Manpower Data Center reports data using the category Individual Ready Reserve/Inactive National Guard. The IRR can be readily disaggregated from this category by subtracting the small figures reported under the subheading Army National Guard (ARNG)—figures that represent the Inactive National Guard portion of the larger category. In 2005 this ARNG portion was reported to number 1,505.

[38] For a discussion of the U.S. military's process for determining officer requirements, see Harry J. Thie, et al., *Future Career Management Systems for U.S. Military Officers*, MR470, RAND Arroyo Center, 1994, http://rand.org/ pubs/monograph_reports/MR470/mr470.ch2.pdf. See also U.S. Congressional Budget Office, "CBO Paper: The Drawdown of the Military Officer Corps," November 1999, http://www.cbo.gov/ftpdocs/17xx/doc1772/drawdown.pdf. The Congressional Budget Office paper discusses how the number and grades of officers are determined in terms of numbers and types of units. The DOD tends to find more general officer requirements than it has Congressional authorizations for. Congress always has an eye on cost and tends to balk at authorizing end strength increases and, especially, to making them relatively permanent by changes to Title 10.

[39] For a discussion of the origins of Title 10 G/FO authorizations for the reserves, see below. As described below, the first mention of a reserve G/FO number ceiling in national legislation, which was in 1958, specified numbers only for the Army. The number, 207 G/FOs, is the same as today's Title 10 limit.

have multiple categories of reserve service. These multiple categories make measures of appropriate officer levels in the reserves more complicated than in the active component. A sizeable part of the reserves, the IIR, is used to "fill in" in undermanned AC or RC units. For example, the service performed by IIR personnel as individual augmentees has different implications for the need for reserve officers than does service as part of a unit. Because of this variety of service in the RC, sheer force size and other measures of magnitude bear a less meaningful and straightforward relationship to the numbers of G/FOs in the reserves than measures of force size do to top officers in the active forces.

In connection with the active components, concerns about AC G/FO levels regularly translate into relatively systematic efforts to see how such levels and changes in them relate to magnitudes or changes in numbers—e.g., numbers of troops or numbers of units—and force structure. In connection with the RC, the consideration of G/FO levels is much more commonly cast in terms of the use—intensity of use—of the reserves, rather than in terms of numbers. Advocates for greater equity for the reserves—e.g., the various associations of reservists—rarely seek to make their case of inadequate or inequitable G/FO strength on the basis of a shortfall in sheer G/FO numbers or a deficiency of numbers in relation to force strength.[40] Such advocates make their case in terms of the degree to which the reserves are being called upon to augment or expand the active-duty force. That is, what matters to reserve advocates in judging appropriate G/FO strength is not so much the baseline size of the reserves as how much they are relied upon. According to reserve advocates, the current intensity of use of the reserves is not being reflected in sufficient institutional power and opportunities for the reserves. The need for more institutional power translates into a push not for larger G/FO numbers but for more top posts—posts above O–8—and for more opportunities for reservists to gain the credentials/experience necessary to compete for such top posts. The main enhanced opportunity that advocates have sought for the reserves is the opportunity to gain joint experience, a prerequisite for top offices since the passage of Pub.L.No. 99–433, the Goldwater–Nichols Defense Reorganization Act of 1986.

---

[40] Some advocacy organizations for the reserves include: the Naval Reserve Association, the National Guard Association, the Naval Enlisted Reserve Association, the Retired Officers Association, the Marine Corps Reserve Officers Association, the Army Reserve Association, and the Enlisted Association of the National Guard.

THE BACKGROUND OF CURRENT G/FO AUTHORIZATIONS IN TITLE 10

The contrast between the AC and RC in their approaches to defining the issue of appropriate G/FO strength has been manifest for several decades in exchanges between the Department of Defense, which identifies officer requirements in its budget requests, and Congress, which passes authorizations. Such exchanges about requirements and authorizations, which have culminated in current congressional G/FO authorizations, are a perennial feature of the U.S budget process.[41] In these exchanges, Congress in its oversight role has repeatedly expressed concern about the officer requirements, including for G/FOs, contained in the DOD's budget requests.[42] Out of a concern with costs, with maintaining adequate promotion opportunities, and with other issues, Congress has periodically mandated studies of G/FO levels—studies that may be DOD-wide, for a specific service, or for the joint community.[43] In issuing such mandates, Congress has typically asked the defense secretary to undertake a review of the number of generals and admirals authorized for the military services and to determine whether there should be more or fewer top-ranked officers.[44] Instances of major congressionally mandated DOD studies of G/FO requirements appeared in 2003, 1997, 1988 (the "Hay Report"), 1978, 1972, and 1966.[45] As the GAO has pointed out, the 1997 study, "according to the DOD …

---

[41] For criteria used in the interactive process between the DOD and Congress in establishing G/FO levels, see U.S. Government Accountability Office (GAO), "Appendix I: Sixteen Factors Used to Validate General and Flag Officer Requirements," *Military Personnel: General and Flag Officer Requirements Are Unclear Based on DOD's 2003 Report to Congress*, GAO–04–488, Washington, DC, April 2004, 29–31, http://www.gao.gov/cgi-bin/getrpt?GAO-04-488.

[42] See, for example, also Major Stephen W. Baird, "Too Many General Officers?," 1991, http://www.globalsecurity.org/military/library/report/1991/BSW.htm.

[43] See U.S. Senate, Committee on Armed Services, Subcommittee on Manpower and Personnel, *General and Flag Officer Requirements*, 100th Cong., 2d sess., August 10, 1988 (statement of Grant Green, Jr., Assistant Secretary of Defense for Force Management and Personnel).

[44] On the major reviews, see GAO, *Military Personnel: General and Flag Officer Requirements Are Unclear Based on DOD's 2003 Report to Congress*, 6.

[45] On the 1966 study, which found a requirement for 1,620 G/FOs, see U.S. Department of Defense, Office of the Assistant Secretary of Defense (Manpower and Reserve Affairs), *Report on General/Flag Officer Requirements*, Washington D C: March 1, 1968, http://stinet.dtic.mil/oai/oai?verb=getRecord&metadataPrefix=html&identifier=AD066885. See also GAO, *Military Personnel: General and Flag Officer Requirements Are Unclear Based on DOD's 2003 Report to Congress*, 6. According to the GAO study, the reports prior to 1997 did not integrate active and reserve component requirements. Thus, when the 1988 Hay Report identified a requirement for 1,436 G/FO positions, it meant AC positions. (At the time, the Title 10 G/FO authorization for the AC was 1,073.) A 1978 DOD study identified a requirement for 1,419 G/FOs. In 1972, DOD identified a requirement for 1,304 G/FOs. Congressional authorizations for general and flag officers typically have been lower than requirements identified in DOD's studies.

was the first to integrate active and reserve component requirements."[46] The 1997 study identified a need for 1,472 G/FOs, including 1,018 active component and 454 reserve component officers.[47] A subsequent study in 2003, responding to a mandate in Pub.L.No. 107–314, section 4049c, the National Defense Authorization Act for Fiscal Year 2003, validated total requirements for 1,630 G/FO positions for the AC and RC combined.[48] In both post-1997 studies, the identified requirements exceeded the total of 1,311 that Congress, since fiscal year 1996, has authorized the services.

Debate about appropriate G/FO strengths has gained intensity in recent years because of a number of post–Cold War changes, mainly, the massive drawdown of the military as a whole and the increased reliance on the reserves to cope with unexpected levels of military operations.[49] These two changes have interacted, producing considerable adjustment pressures in both the AC and RC. Heavier reliance on the reserves began prior to the end of the Cold War—with the cessation of the draft in 1973—but remained relatively moderate in its impact on operational tempo until the 1990s, because the active forces were generally maintained at high levels during the Cold War's last decade.[50] During the same decade of the 1980s, the reserves saw an enormous peacetime buildup. The Selected Reserve, the main part of the Ready Reserve, grew by 35 percent between 1980 and 1989, because of the DOD's total force policy, which placed an increasing emphasis on the reserve force.[51] With the end of the Cold War, both the AC and the RC experienced significant downsizing, with the cuts in reserve end strength—both enlisted and officer—less severe than the cuts in the active component end strength.[52] The drawdown of the AC between 1990 and 2005, with force totals and a breakdown of officer and enlisted numbers, is shown in Table 11 below.

---

[46] GAO, *Military Personnel: General and Flag Officer Requirements Are Unclear Based on DOD's 2003 Report to Congress*, 6.
[47] GAO, *Military Personnel: General and Flag Officer Requirements Are Unclear Based on DOD's 2003 Report to Congress*, 6.
[48] U.S. Department of Defense, Office of the Under Secretary of Defense, Personnel and Readiness, *Review of Active Duty and Reserve General and Flag Officer Authorizations*, Washington, DC, March 31, 2003.
[49] U.S Congress, House of Representatives, Committee on National Security, Subcommittee on Military Personnel, *Hearings on National Defense Authorization Act for FY 1998: HR 1119 and Oversight of Previously Authorized Programs*, 105th Cong., 1st sess., April 8, 1997.
[50] Beth J. Asch, *Reserve Supply in the Post-Desert Storm Recruiting Environment* (Santa Monica: Rand, 1993), 3, http://www.rand.org/pubs/monograph_reports/2006/MR224.pdf.
[51] Asch, 3.
[52] Asch, 4. As noted below, during the 1990s drawdown of reserve officers, G/FO authorizations for the reserves did not change.

Table 11. Active Component: 1990 to 2005

Rank/Grade	*1990*	*1995*	*2000*	*2002*	*2003*	*2004*	*2005*
Total	**2,043,700**	**1,518,200**	**1,384,300**	**1,411,600**	**1,434,400**	**1,426,800**	**1,389,400**
Total Officers (incl. warrant)	296,600	237,600	217,200	223,000	227,900	226,700	226,600
Total Enlisted	1,733,800	1,268,500	1,154,600	1,176,200	1,193,900	1,172,000	1,149,900

Source: U.S. Department of Defense, *Official Guard and Reserve Manpower Strengths and Statistics,* quarterly. See also U.S. Department of Defense, Defense Manpower Data Center, Statistical Information Analysis Division, http://siadapp.dior.whs.mil/index.html.

As Table 11 shows, the downsizing of the active force from its Cold War high was accompanied by a similarly significant officer strength reduction. Between 1989 and 1996, the Department of Defense reduced the number of officers on active duty by 23 percent as part of the post–Cold War drawdown of military personnel.[53]

The overall force drawdown of the reserves and reductions in specific services are shown in Table 12 below.

Table 12. Reserve Personnel: 1990 to 2005

Reserve status and branch of service	*1990*	*1995*	*2000*	*2002*	*2003*	*2004*	*2005*
Total reserves (less retired reserves)	**1,688,674**	**1,674,164**	**1,276,843**	**1,222,337**	**1,188,851**	**1,166,937**	**1,136,200**
Ready reserve	*1,658,707*	*1,648,388*	*1,251,452*	*1,199,321*	*1,167,101*	*1,145,035*	*1,113,427*
Army (Guard and Reserve)	1,049,579	999,462	725,771	699,548	682,522	663,209	636,355
Navy	240,228	267,356	184,080	159,098	152,855	148,643	140,821
Marine Corps	81,355	103,668	99,855	97,944	98,868	101,443	99,820
Air Force (Guard and Reserve)	270,313	263,011	229,009	229,798	219,895	219,159	223,551
Coast Guard	17,232	14,891	12,737	12,933	12,961	12,581	12,880
Standby reserve	*29,967*	*25,776*	*25,391*	*23,016*	*21,750*	*21,902*	*22,773*
Retired reserve	*462,371*	*505,905*	*573,305*	*590,018*	*601,611*	*614,904*	*627,424*

Source: U.S. Department of Defense, *Official Guard and Reserve Manpower Strengths and Statistics*, quarterly. See also U.S. Department of Defense, Defense Manpower Data Center, Statistical Information Analysis Division, http://siadapp.dior.whs.mil/index.html.

---

[53] Congressional Budget Office, 1.

Within the RC, the two branches of the National Guard saw relatively modest reductions of overall personnel between 1990 and 2005 and actual increases in the numbers of units, as shown in Table 13 below:

Table 13. National Guard—Summary: 1980 to 2005

Item		*1980*	*1990*	*1995*	*2000*	*2001*	*2002*	*2003*	*2004*	*2005*
ARNG										
Units	Number	3,379	4,005	5,872	5,300	5,200	5,150	5,100	*5,100	5,000
	Personnel in 1,000s	368	444	375	353	352	352	351	343	334
ANG										
Units	Number	1,054	1,339	1,604	1,550	1,500	1,500	1,500	*1,500	*1,400
	Personnel in 1,000s	96	118	110	106	109	112	108	108	106

Source: Based on U.S Census Bureau, *Statistical Abstract of the United States: 2007,* 335, http://www.census.gov/prod/2006pubs/07statab/defense.pdf.

Historical Snapshot of AC G/FO Authorizations Since World War II

The post–Cold War drawdown was accompanied by G/FO reductions and, until the latest revision of Title 10 of G/FO number ceilings in 1996, by decreases in G/FO authorizations. As the drawdown was anticipated and proceeded, Congress revised downward the Title 10 G/FO authorizations for the active component, while leaving constant those it had recently established for the reserve component. In Pub.L.No. 101–510, the National Defense Authorization Act for Fiscal Year 1991, Congress required DOD to reduce its AC general and flag officer positions in two increments, first from 1,073—the congressionally authorized ceiling since October 1, 1981—to 1,030 by the end of fiscal year 1994 and secondly to 858 by the beginning of fiscal year 1995. That number was subsequently changed to 865.[54] When 12 G/FO positions were added for the Marine Corps in 1996, the authorized numbers in Title 10 reached their current baseline level.[55] The addition of the Chairman's 12 in 1997 brought the actual authorized G/FO positions available to the active military to 889.

---

[54] U.S. General Accounting Office (GAO), *General and Flag Officers: Number Required is Unclear Based on DOD's Draft Report,* GAO/NSIAD–97–160, Washington, DC, June 1997, 2, http://www.gao.gov/archive/1997/ns97160.pdf.
[55] See GAO, *General And Flag Officers: DOD's Study Needs Adjustments: Testimony Before the Subcommittee on Military Personnel, Committee on National Security, House of Representatives,* GAO/T–NSIAD–97–122, April 8, 1997, 2, http://www.gao.gov/archive/1997/ns97122t.pdf.

The fluctuations in AC G/FO authorizations seen since the 1980s are a continuation of the characteristic pattern of the U.S. military, which is subject to a cycle of buildup and drawdown mostly determined by major events affecting national security. Changes in G/FO authorizations track these ups and downs of the force, albeit imperfectly and often with time lags. In 1945, as World War II ended, active-duty general and flag officer positions stood at a high of more than 2,000.[56] At that time, the active military had nearly 12 million members, with some 1.1 million officers.[57] Then followed the post–World War II demobilization in the late 1940s. As each service was in the process of scaling down its general officer strength from World War II highs, the Officer Personnel Act (OPA) of 1947 established limits on the authorized number of general/flag officers for each service. By 1951, actual AC G/FO numbers had fallen to about 1,000 for all services combined. The Korean War prompted a military buildup in the early 1950s, including a rise in G/FO numbers. Following the Korean War, the Officer Grade Level Act (OGLA) of 1954 fixed ceilings that codified in law the significant growth of G/FO numbers between 1950 and 1954. In the years following the 1954 OGLA, 1955 to 1965, congressional authorizations for the U.S. military, including officers, were relatively stable for the Navy and Marine Corps, while the Army experienced modest growth and the Air Force expanded significantly.[58] The Vietnam conflict brought another era of growth and drawdown. In order to support that conflict, the Senate in 1965 authorized an increase in G/FO authorizations for all the services. In 1967 DOD had about 1,300 authorized active-duty general and flag officers.[59] Total uniformed personnel, including enlisted personnel and officers, exceeded 2.5 million in 1964, falling by 1976 to 2.052 million.[60]

Subsequent to the Vietnam conflict, i.e., after 1975, the military's G/FO authorizations were again reduced, reaching 1,141 by 1976. The National Defense Authorization Act for Fiscal Year 1978 directed a reduction of 6 percent in the total number of G/FOs throughout the Department of Defense (DOD).[61] This legislation reduced the number of G/FOs from 1,141 to 1,073, a total reduction of 68 G/FOs. The reason for the 6 percent reduction, as in previous

---

[56] GAO, *General And Flag Officers: Number Required Is Unclear Based On DOD's Draft Report*, 2. See also Thie and Marquis, 2.
[57] Thie and Marquis, 2.
[58] Thie and Marquis, 2.
[59] GAO, *General And Flag Officers: Number Required Is Unclear Based On DOD's Draft Report*, 2.
[60] See Appendix 1 below.
[61] U.S. Army, Center of Military History, "Manning the Army," chapter 5 in *Army Historical Summary: Fiscal Year 1980*, http://www.army.mil/CMH/books/DAHSUM/1980/ch05.htm.

drawdowns, was the belief in Congress that there were too many generals and admirals in the DOD.[62] The reduction was phased in over several years with the final reduction to 1,073 G/FOs directed in the FY82 defense authorization act, the number ceiling that remained in effect for a decade, i.e., until the defense authorization act of 1991 took effect.[63] At the same time that the number of AC G/FO authorizations held steady for a decade at 1,073, the size of the military as a whole saw a significant increase during the Reagan administration's military buildup.[64] Total AC personnel numbered 2.051 million in 1981, peaked at 2.141 million in 1987, and fell to 1.952 million in 1991.[65]

Throughout the post–World War II decades, the dramatic fluctuations in force numbers did not affect all the services equally and did not translate into exactly proportional changes in the sizes of the officer corps at various grades. At all times, the services in the active component differ greatly in size and vary considerably in their ratio of enlisted to officer personnel. Figure 1 shows the AC strength by service and the number of officers and enlisted in each. The Army is the largest service, the Marine Corps the smallest.[66]

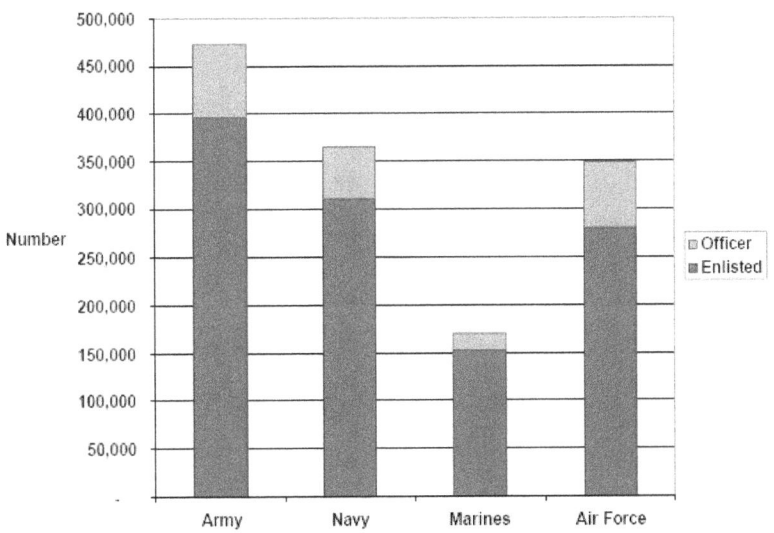

Figure 1. Size of Active Component, May 2001

Source: Based on Harry J. Thie and Jefferson P. Marquis, *The Present Military Personnel Management Framework: Where It Came From*, PM–1247–OSD, September 2001, http://www.defenselink.mil/prhome/docs/military_hr_stratplan3.pdf.

---

[62] U.S. Army, Center of Military History, *Army Historical Summary: Fiscal Year 1980.*
[63] GAO, *General And Flag Officers: DOD's Study Needs Adjustments: Testimony*, 2.
[64] Asch, 4.
[65] See Appendix 1 in this report.
[66] Thie and Marquis, 3.

In the military's cycle of buildup and drawdown, the Army has always seen the most dramatic changes. During both Korea and Vietnam, the Army was more than three times as large as it is was by 2000.[67] After those two conflicts, it dropped to about 1.5 times its size in 2000. The size of the Navy and especially the Marine Corps, by contrast, has historically remained relatively stable. Figure 2 highlights AC size differences over the last 50 years for each service, by showing size as a percentage of size in 2000.

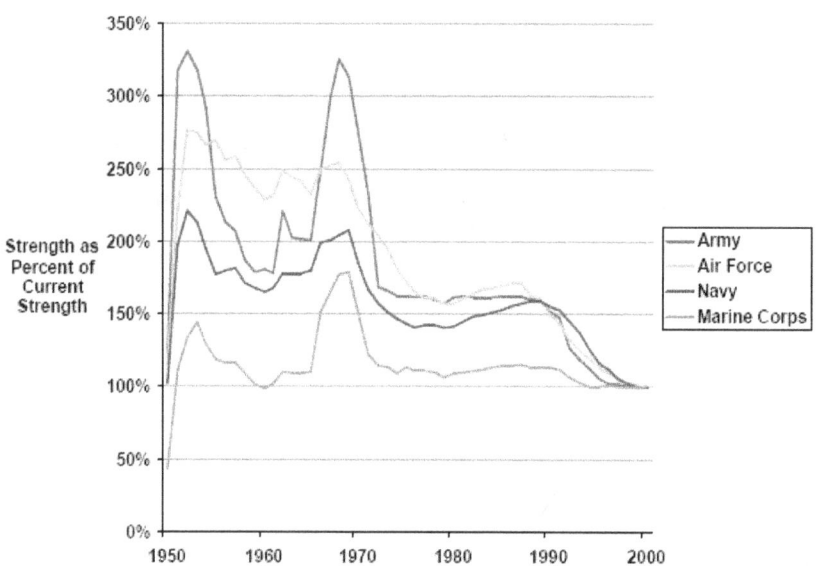

Figure 2. Service Strength (1950–2000) as a Percentage of 2000 Strength

Source: Based on Harry J. Thie and Jefferson P. Marquis, *The Present Military Personnel Management Framework: Where It Came From*, PM–1247–OSD, September 2001, http://www.defenselink.mil/prhome/docs/military_hr_stratplan3.pdf.

Because the overall force strength of the services fluctuates, while authorized officer strengths are slower to change, the ratio of enlisted to officer personnel rises and falls somewhat over time. The enlisted-to-officer ratio also varies considerably among the services. In 2000, for instance, the enlisted-to-officer ratio varied from about 9:1 in the Marine Corps to 6:1 in the Navy, 5:1 in the Army, and 4:1 in the Air Force.[68]

For all the fluctuations in the E–O ratio over time and the variations among the services, however, the long-term tendency in the U.S. military has been for the E–O ratio to decline, and for the average grade in each service to rise, reflecting a general shift from enlisted to officer

---

[67] Thie and Marquis, 2.

manpower. Between 1950 and 2000, as shown in Figure 3, the E–O ratio trended downward in all of the services, while the differences in the ratios among the services remained relatively constant.

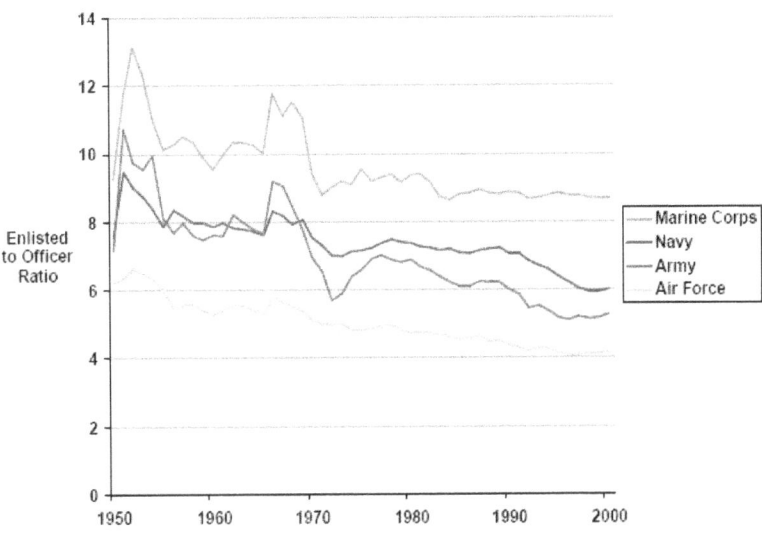

Figure 3. Ratio of Enlisted to Officer (1950–2000)

Source: Based on Harry J. Thie and Jefferson P. Marquis, *The Present Military Personnel Management Framework: Where It Came From*, PM–1247–OSD, September 2001, http://www.defenselink.mil/prhome/docs/military_hr_stratplan3.pdf.

The long-term trend continued throughout the 1990s drawdown, despite the declared aim of Congress to hold the E–O ratios constant at the 1990 level.[69] Although the number of officers fell in each of the services during the post–Cold War drawdown, officers came to represent a larger proportion of the AC force. Only the Marine Corps reduced its officer corps by as large a percentage as its enlisted force.[70] As a result, it was the only service in which the ratio of enlisted to officer personnel did not decline.[71] The Army's ratio experienced the greatest decline, from 6.2 in 1989 to 5.0 in 1996, a drop of 19 percent.[72] The ratios in the Air Force and Navy fell by 11 percent and 14 percent, respectively, as shown in Table 14.

---

[68] Thie and Marquis, 2.
[69] GAO, *Military Personnel: High Aggregate Personnel Levels Maintained Throughout Drawdown*, GAO/NSIAD–95–97, Washington, DC, June 1995, 5, http://archive.gao.gov/t2pbat1/154251.pdf.
[70] Congressional Budget Office, 32.
[71] Congressional Budget Office, 31.
[72] Congressional Budget Office, 31.

Table 14. Ratio of Enlisted to Officer Personnel, By Service, Fiscal Years 1989–1996

	Army	Air Force	Navy	Marine Corps	All Services
1989	6.2	4.5	7.2	8.8	6.0
1990	6.0	4.3	7.0	8.9	5.8
1991	5.8	4.2	7.0	8.8	5.8
1992	5.4	4.2	6.8	8.6	5.6
1993	5.5	4.2	6.6	8.7	5.6
1994	5.3	4.2	6.5	8.8	5.5
1995	5.1	4.1	6.3	8.8	5.3
1996	5.0	4.0	6.2	8.8	5.3
Percentage Decline, 1989–1996	19	11	14	0	12
Source: U.S. Congressional Budget Office, "CBO Paper: The Drawdown of the Military Officer Corps," November 1999, http://www.cbo.gov/ftpdocs/17xx/doc1772/ drawdown.pdf. Based on data from the U.S. Department of Defense, http://www.cbo. gov/ftpdocs/17xx/doc1772/drawdown.pdf.					

The pay-grade growth over the past 50 years, as seen among commissioned officers, is shown in Figure 4.

Figure 4. Average Commissioned Officer Grade, 1958–2000

Source: Based on Harry J. Thie and Jefferson P. Marquis, *The Present Military Personnel Management Framework: Where It Came From*, PM–1247–OSD, September 2001, http://www.defenselink.mil/prhome/docs/military_hr_stratplan3.pdf.

The pay-grade growth that affected all ranks—enlisted and officer—disproportionately affected the topmost ranks of the officer corps, i.e., above O–7.[73] During the 1990s drawdown, "grade creep" manifested itself in the way officer reductions occurred. In all services except the Navy, the percentage decline of officers above grade O–7 was smaller than the decline of the commissioned officer corps as a whole, as shown in Table 15.

Table 15. Change in Numbers of G/FOs and All Commissioned Officers, FY 1989–96

	Number 1989	Number 1996	Percentage Change	Current Title 10 Authorization (including Chairman's 12)
All Services				
G/FOs	1,066	855	–19.8	877 + 12
O–1–O–10	283,540	216,990	–23.5	
Army				
G/FOs	407	308	–24.3	302 + 5
O–1–O–10	91,900	68,971	–24.9	
Air Force				
G/FOs	333	275	–17.4	279 + 3
O–1–O–10	103,699	76,389	–26.4	
Navy				
G/FOs	256	204	–20.3	216 + 4
O–1–O–10	69,475	55,602	–20.0	
Marine Corps				
G/FOs	70	68	–2.9	80
O–1–O–10	18,466	16,028	–13.2	
Source: U.S. Congressional Budget Office, "CBO Paper: The Drawdown of the Military Officer Corps," November 1999, http://www.cbo.gov/ftpdocs/17xx/doc1772/drawdown.pdf. Based on data from the U.S. Department of Defense, 28, http://www.cbo.gov/ftpdocs/17xx/doc1772/drawdown.pdf.				

Periodically over the last several decades, the Congress, in its concern about costs, has questioned the trend toward a more highly graded military, often voicing the suspicion that the services found it easier to separate enlisted personnel than officers, especially senior officers.[74] Congressional and other critics frequently have cited decreases in the services' E–O ratios as handy evidence of an unnecessarily officer-heavy force.[75]

---

[73] Congressional Budget Office, 2.
[74] Congressional Budget Office, 32.
[75] Major Scott T. Nestler, "Officer Bloat or Changing Requirements?" *Army Magazine*, February 1, 2004, http://www.ausa.org/webpub/DeptArmyMagazine.nsf/byid/CCRN-6CCSBW.

In responding to the concerns of Congress, those who have campaigned for increased authorizations for officers at various ranks have been obliged to explain and justify why the military's E–O ratio has changed. The services have argued that decreases in the enlisted-to-officer ratio have been justified by changing requirements for personnel.[76] Addressing broad and long-term causes of change, they argue that changing requirements are a result of new technologies and military doctrines that have decreased the need for enlisted personnel relative to the need for officers. Addressing more proximate causes of change, the services most often cite new requirements for officers in joint-service assignments.[77] The services have been asked increasingly to provide officers for joint positions. The joint community, which needs no congressional approval to change the number of G/FOs it requires, merely levies its ever-growing requirements on the services.[78] The demand to fill joint billets has created the requirement for more G/FOs and, as one witness before Congress in 1998 put it, the need "for some increases in current limits on Active and Reserve component general and flag officers."[79] The witness, quoting a Marine Corps report, further said,

> As articulated by the Marine Corps last year, the fundamental reason for the need to increase the numbers of general and flag officers was that, "The unconstrained growth of the number of joint and external general and flag officer requirements and the growing need for services to fill those positions has left the services, whose available pool of general and flag officers is tightly constrained, unable to fill both external and internal service requirements."[80]

In addition to increased joint-duty requirements, a further recent source of increased demands for AC G/FOs is the requirement that the services assign some AC officers to command reserve units. Intended to improve reserve component training and to increase active-reserve integration, this requirement has strained the AC's capacity to meet its own requirements for G/FOs, because Congress has not authorized additional AC G/FOs for assignment to the reserves.[81]

Whatever the reasons for "grade creep," "top-sizing," or the changing proportion of enlisted to officer personnel, the debate about them is ongoing and, in connection with the AC,

---

[76] See U.S. House of Representatives, *National Defense Authorization Act for Fiscal Year 1987,* conference report to accompany S. 2638, H.Rep.No. 99–661, November 14, 1986.

[77] U.S. Department of Defense, *Defense Officer Requirements Study,* March 1988, 32–36.

[78] GAO, *General And Flag Officers: DOD's Study Needs Adjustments: Testimony,* 3.

[79] *Hearings on National Defense Authorization Act for FY 1998.*

[80] *Hearings on National Defense Authorization Act for FY 1998.*

continues frequently to be carried out with reference to longitudinal comparisons of E–O ratios. In connection with the AC, such ratios are relatively easy to calculate and to track over time, enabling analysts to draw an historical picture of fluctuations of officer strength and to identify long-term trends.

Historical Snapshot of RC G/FO Authorizations Since World War II

Although an historical picture of the actual and authorized G/FO levels over time can be drawn for the active component, the establishment of a similar picture for the reserve component is far more challenging and has proven to be of less interest to analysts and policymakers. The statutory control of reserve officer management, including the specification of number ceilings for officers at various grades, was slow to develop and long remained comparatively general. Up to and for some years after World War II, matters concerning reserve officers, such as promotion, were addressed only through service-specific regulations. When the end of World War II brought heightened concern with officer management to the U.S. military, most attention focused on the active component, with, for example, the Officer Personnel Act (OPA) of 1947. This act did not address reserve officers very specifically and was quite general across all of the services. The Armed Forces Reserve Act, which was enacted in 1952, provided the first major legislation that formed a basis for reserve personnel management. In 1954 an act concerning reserve officers, the Reserve Officer Personnel Act (ROPA), was enacted. ROPA provided statutory procedures for reserve officer personnel management but imposed little uniformity on major elements of the reserve officer promotion process and did not specifically address G/FOs or G/FO numbers. A search of Title 10 indicates that a section of the U.S. Code on reserve G/FO authorizations was first added through legislation in 1958, specifically through Pub.L.No. 85–861, section 3218 of September 2, 1958. Section 3218 of Pub.L.No. 85–861 specified the number ceiling for G/FOs in the Army's reserve components. The section, "Reserves: strength in grade; general officers in active status," read as follows:

> The authorized strength of the Army in reserve general officers in an active status, exclusive of those serving as adjutants general or assistant adjutants general of a State or Territory, Puerto Rico, the Canal Zone, or the District of Columbia, and those serving in the National Guard Bureau, is 207.[82]

---

[81] GAO, *Military Personnel: High Aggregate Personnel Levels Maintained Throughout Drawdown*, 36.
[82] Pub.L.No. 85–861, 72 Stat 1437, 1463, September 2, 1958.

The limit on G/FOs imposed by section 3218 was the same as the current limit for the Army that Title 10, section 12004, now specifies. The wording of section 3218 remained in force until 1994 with only minor changes, such as the elimination of the mention of the Canal Zone. The section wording was replaced on October 5, 1994, by Pub.L.No. 103–337, the National Defense Authorization Act of FY95, which substituted section 12004, the Title 10 section as currently numbered, that covers reserve G/FO numbers for all of the services, and not just the Army. Pub.L.No. 103–337 included Title XVI, the Reserve Officer Personnel Management Act (ROPMA), the first comprehensive overhaul and update of the reserve officer personnel management statutes since the enactment of ROPA in 1954.

ROPMA revised the structure of Title 10, consolidating the provisions relating to the RC.[83] ROPMA, which provided promotion guidelines and limits, addressed mandatory separation, and tightened standards, etc., served as a supplement for the reserves to the Defense Officer Personnel Management Act (DOPMA) of 1980.[84] DOPMA, the first major revision of officer management since the OPA of 1947, was mainly enacted for the active component, although it had resolved some issues of promotion for the reserves. ROPMA superceded numerous regulations that had governed reserve officer personnel management, for example, some 17 major regulations in the Army.[85] ROPMA unified all the services with respect to their management of the reserve officers and helped align the reserves with their parent services, thereby advancing the concept of the Total Force.[86]

The Road to the Third Star For the Reserve and Guard Leadership

The fact that statutory control of reserve personnel, and particularly legislation on G/FOs, was slow to develop does not mean that G/FOs have not been an issue of interest to reserve advocates. It is just that the concern with G/FOs has not primarily involved a preoccupation with

---

[83] The Reserve Officer Personnel Management Act (ROPMA), "Chain Teaching Package" on ROPMA including a Program of Instruction (POI) in Microsoft Word (52KB) and a Microsoft PowerPoint (113KB) presentation, http://www.delahunty.com/infantry/ropma.ppt.
[84] Sue Cathcart and Christopher Prawdzik, "ROPMA: Challenged, Some Officers Excel Under New Rules," *National Guard* 56, no. 6 (July 2002): 28–30.
[85] Army regulations that ROPMA superceded included, among others: AR 135–18, The Active Guard Reserve (AGR) Program; AR 140–30, Army Reserve—Active Duty in Support of the United States Army Reserve and Active Guard Reserve Management Program; AR 135–155, Promotion of Commissioned Officers and Warrant Officers Other Than General Officers; AR 135–100, Appointment of Commissioned and Warrant Officers of the Army; and AR 135–175, ARNG and USAR—Separation of Officers. See ROPMA, "Chain Teaching Package."
[86] ROPMA does not apply to warrant officers.

G/FO numbers and number authorizations. Reserve concerns have primarily centered, rather, on the grades of specific billets of the top leadership and on opportunities for officers to acquire qualifications—especially, joint-duty qualifications—for promotion to higher grades. As for numbers, the earliest mention in law of reserve G/FO numbers was in 1958 in the act that specified a G/FO ceiling of 207 for the Army reserve components, a number that still stands in Title 10. Number ceilings added after ROPMA for the other services have also remained unchanged up to the present, notwithstanding some proposals to raise the ceilings. In 1997, for example, a draft DOD report recommended that RC G/FO positions be increased by 32, to 454 (632, including the 178 general officers serving as state adjutants general or assistant adjutants general or in the National Guard Bureau).[87] The proposed ceilings, as well as the pre-1997 ceilings, which remain unrevised up to the present, are shown in Table 16.

Table 16. Current and Draft Ceiling on Reserve Component G/FOs

Service	Pre-1997 ceiling	Proposed ceiling	Increase
Army	207	227	20
Navy	48	53	5
Air Force	157	161	4
Marine Corps	10	13	3
Total	**422**	**454**	**32**

Source: Based on U.S.C. Title 10 and U.S. General Accounting Office (GAO), *General And Flag Officers: Number Required Is Unclear Based On DOD's Draft Report*, GAO/NSIAD–97–160, Washington, DC, June 1997, http://www.gao.gov/archive/1997/ns97160.pdf.

In proposing such increases in the reserve G/FO number ceilings, DOD argued that the statutory limits then in effect did not adequately recognize the increased role of the reserve components in operations.[88] DOD also offered the same argument most often advanced in favor of increasing the authorizations for active-duty G/FOs, namely, that the demand for officers to fill joint-duty positions has increased.[89] As one DOD spokesperson said about a proposal to increase Marine Corps Reserve G/FO billets from 10 to 16,

---

[87] U.S. General Accounting Office (GAO), *General And Flag Officers: Number Required Is Unclear Based On DOD's Draft Report*, GAO/NSIAD–97–160, June 1997, 11, http://www.gao.gov/archive/1997/ns97160.pdf.
[88] GAO, *General And Flag Officers: Number Required Is Unclear Based On DOD's Draft Report*, 11.
[89] U.S. Department of Defense, Office of the Assistant Secretary of Defense (Public Affairs), *National Guard, Reserve—Central Parts of Total Force: Prepared Statement of Deborah R. Lee, Assistant Secretary of Defense for Reserve Affairs*, Testimony before the Readiness Subcommittee, Senate Armed Services Committee, February 6, 1996 (also posted as *Defense Issues*: Volume 11, Number 23), http://www.defenselink.mil/speeches/speech.aspx?speechid=874.

> I am advised that the need to provide reserve expertise and perspectives on the capabilities, roles and missions of reserve forces in the joint arena has led to an increase in the requirements for reserve general and flag officers to serve on the staffs of combatant commanders.[90]

Similar arguments about the numbers of G/FOs have been offered by reserve advocates in Congress, for example, in 1999, by Senator Jeff Sessions, a long-time advocate for the reserves.[91] In testimony about the G/FO situation of the reserves, he made passing reference to inequity between the active and reserve components in terms of sheer numbers. However, neither such passing complaints nor earlier DOD recommendations ultimately redounded to any change in Title 10 numbers, in part because the issue of sheer numbers, even for consistent reserve advocates such as Sessions, was at best a secondary concern. Although advocates for changes in reserve G/FO authorizations have favored increased overall numbers, they have concentrated on grade increases. The lack of preoccupation with overall number ceilings in discussions of officer strength in the RC has translated into a dearth of references to the enlisted–to–officer ratios in the reserves. Advocates for the reserves have expended the bulk of their energy in efforts to ensure that the top leadership of the reserves gained the opportunity to achieve positions above O–8.

The first achievement in efforts to elevate the grade of top RC officers occurred in 1979, when the chief of the National Guard Bureau (CNGB) was statutorily accorded three-star rank.[92] Another two decades passed before other officers of the reserve components were accorded three stars, namely, in 2000, when three-star positions were finally mandated for the reserve chiefs and National Guard directors. Prior to that time, the highest ranked reserve officers, apart from the CNGB, were two star officers. Pub.L.No. 106–398, National Defense Authorization Act for Fiscal Year 2001, section 507, "Grade of Chiefs of Reserve Components and Directors of National Guard Components." enacted in October 2000, directed that the reserve chiefs—Army, Navy, Air Force, and Marine Corps—and directors of Guard components—Army and Air

---

[90] U.S. Department of Defense, Office of the Assistant Secretary of Defense (Public Affairs), *National Guard, Reserve—Central Parts of Total Force: Prepared Statement of Deborah R. Lee, Assistant Secretary of Defense for Reserve Affairs.*

[91] U.S. Congress, Senate, Senate Floor State of Senator Sessions: Sessions Amendment No. 465 Offered To S. 1059, National Defense Authorization Act of Fiscal Year 2000, May 27, 1999, http://sessions.senate.gov/pressapp/record.cfm?id=178423.

[92] With the elevation of the CNGB position from major general to lieutenant general in 1979, the incumbent Chief of the National Guard Bureau, who had been appointed to the position in 1974, received a third star. Five other chiefs have since held this rank and office. In 1988 the position of vice chief, NGB was created and filled with a major general.

Force—be promoted to O–9 not later than 12 months after the law's enactment. In addition, Pub.L.No. 106–398 extended the authority to waive until October 1, 2003, on a case-by-case basis, the joint-service prerequisite for promotion for those officers nominated for appointment as one of the reserve chiefs. In June 2001, a number of the promotions mandated by Pub.L.No. 106–398 took place, when the chief, Army Reserve, and the director, Army National Guard, were sworn in as lieutenant generals by the chief of staff of the Army.[93]

This authorization of additional positions for reserve G/FOs above O–8 and the designation of the chief and director positions as three-star billets were the culmination of a more than decade-long campaign by reserve advocates, such as the Reserve Officers Association (ROA) and various members of Congress. The need for additional positions above O–8 was argued throughout the decade of the 1990s. In 1989 a study by General William Richardson went so far as to recommend elevation of the chief of the Army Reserve, to four-star rank.[94] That recommendation accompanied a proposal in the same study to restructure the chain of command in the Army through the establishment of a separate Army Reserve Command under the chief of the Army Reserve.[95] Up until that time, command and control authority over the Army Reserve forces had lain with the regular Army, specifically, with the U.S. Army Forces Command (FORSCOM). Section 903 of the National Defense Authorization Act for Fiscal Year 1991, enacted in November 1990, seconded the recommendation of the Richardson study concerning a new command, when the act directed the establishment of the United States Army Reserve Command under the command of the chief of the Army Reserve.[96]

In 1992 the Hay Group, Incorporated, a contractor specializing in job analysis, presented a study on G/FOs in the RC to the assistant secretary of defense for reserve affairs. The study, which had been called for in the conference report that accompanied the defense authorization acts for fiscal years 1990 and 1991, reviewed all DOD requirements for, and distributions of, RC G/FO billets.[97] The study advocated upgrading five positions to O–9, the chiefs of the Army, Air

---

[93] Lt. Col. Randy Pullen, "Army Reserve's Long Fight Wins a Three-Star CAR," *Washington Update: Senior Army Reserve Commanders Association* 20, no. 2 (July 2001): 1, http://sarca.us/News/update-0107.pdf.

[94] Colonel Frank Edens, "The Chronology of Obtaining a Three-Star CAR and Establishing an Army Reserve Command," *Washington Update: Senior Army Reserve Commanders Association* 20, no. 2 (July 2001): 6, http://sarca.us/News/update-0107.pdf.

[95] U.S. Army. Center of Military History, "Reserve Components," chapter 8 in *Army Historical Summary: Fiscal Year 1989*, 141, http://www.army.mil/cmh-pg/books/DAHSUM/1989/CH8.htm.

[96] Pub.L.No. 101–510, *National Defense Authorization Act for Fiscal Year 1999*, Title IX, 104 Stat 1485, 1620, November 5, 1990.

[97] Edens, 6.

Force, and Naval Reserves and the directors of the Army and Air Force National Guard.[98] The study did not include a recommendation to raise the rank of the chief of the Marine Corps Reserve to three stars. The Hay Group report did address the issue of whether reserve G/FOs should count against the active-duty number ceiling imposed by sections 525 and 526 of Title 10, U.S. Code. The group suggested that counting reserve officers against the active-duty ceilings had the potential to set up competition between the active force and the reserve force for the scarce resource of G/FO authorizations.[99] The Hay report concluded that a separate ceiling or separate management of the full-time reserve G/FO billets would provide a better management process. DOD chose to make no recommendations when it submitted the 1992 Hay Study to Congress and, for the next several years, did not take steps to implement the study's findings, despite further advocacy and reinforcing studies.[100]

Further studies supporting the findings of the Hay Group on RC G/FOs included a report by the U.S Army Reserve Command Independent Commission, an independent commission chaired by General John Foss, USA (Ret). That report recommended elevating the rank of the chief of the Army Reserve to lieutenant general, as well as establishing United States Army Reserve Command as a Major United States Army Command (MACOM). In January 1993, the Secretary of the Army commented before Congress on the commission's recommendations, observing,

> The Army agrees with the Commission that the responsibilities and scope of function of the USARC Commander equate to a valid three-star requirement, and therefore I have approved its recognition as a three star position. The Commission also recommended that we fill the position immediately at the three star level, and we are not yet able to make that commitment. Our ability to support the lieutenant general requirement must be determined as part of an overall review of three and four star requirements within the Army…we must let the dust settle a bit before making a decision to fill the three star requirement.[101]

In addition to various studies on reserve G/FOs and related issues, the mid-1990s saw congressional hearings that touched on such issues, for example, hearings before the House National Security Subcommittee on Personnel on H.R. 1646, Reserve Forces Bill of Rights and Revitalization Act. In a hearing on February 6, 1996, Deborah R. Lee, assistant secretary of

---

[98] Edens, 6.
[99] Edens, 6.
[100] U.S. Department of Defense, Office of the Assistant Secretary of Defense (Public Affairs), *National Guard, Reserve—Central Parts of Total Force: Prepared Statement of Deborah R. Lee.*

defense for reserve affairs, testified in support of proposals to upgrade the reserves' top officers, stressing the greater role that the reserves now have:

> Although it is difficult to support proposed grade increases during a downsizing of the force, I believe that the numbers and grades of general and flag officers supporting the reserve command establishment may need to be reviewed on the basis of the relative size of the reserve force within the total force and the increased responsibilities inherent in the missions being assigned to that force. Reserve forces are no longer follow-on forces. They are now an integral element in nearly all military operations—peacetime, wartime, contingency operations and operations other than war.[102]

In addition to supporting pay-grade increases, she also concurred with the 1992 Hay Group report in advocating the exemption of reserve general/flag officer positions from statutory active-duty pay-grade ceilings.

By 1997 the hitherto inconclusive discussions about elevating the ranks of the top reserve officers had prompted Congress to order that this topic of reserve ranks be specifically addressed in a broad review of G/FO authorizations. Pub.L.No. 104–201, the National Defense Authorization Act for Fiscal Year 1997, directed the secretary of defense to provide Congress with a full evaluation—"a comprehensive review"—of all general officer positions.[103] This report was to be the most comprehensive on G/FOs since a 1988 DOD-wide study by the Hay Group had examined G/FO requirements in the AC.[104] In fact, the 1997 report was to be the most comprehensive ever on the topic of G/FO requirements, in that the study was to be the first to integrate active and reserve component requirements.[105] The 1997 congressional requirement for a report on G/FOs arose out of opposition in Congress to an effort by the Marine Corps in 1996 to increase the number of general officers from 68 to 80.[106] Members in the House and Senate, both opponents and advocates of the Marine Corps increase, suggested looking at different

---

[101] Edens, 6.

[102] U.S. Department of Defense, Office of the Assistant Secretary of Defense (Public Affairs), *National Guard, Reserve—Central Parts of Total Force: Prepared Statement of Deborah R. Lee.*

[103] See Pub.L.No. 104–201, *National Defense Authorization Act for Fiscal Year 1997*, sections 1213(b) through (e). DOD developed a draft report in response to this requirement; however, it never issued a final report.

[104] See GAO, *Military Personnel: General and Flag Officer Requirements Are Unclear Based on DOD's 2003 Report to Congress*, 6. The 1988 Hay Report identified a requirement for 1,436 general and flag officer positions in the AC.

[105] GAO, *Military Personnel: General and Flag Officer Requirements Are Unclear Based on DOD's 2003 Report to Congress*, 6.

[106] Woody West, "Old Story, New Title; No Time for Generals –Questionable Need for More Marine Generals and Navy Admirals," *Insight on the News,* November 4, 1996, http://findarticles.com/p/articles/mi_m1571/is_n41_v12/ai_18822628.

aspects of what Senator Charles Grassley of Iowa, called "topsizing"—increasing the number of top brass at a time when all the services and the rest of the government were downsizing.[107] As one opponent to such increases said, "Headquarters should not be growing as the force shrinks."[108] In seeking a broad review of G/FOs, the legislators also charged the GAO with assessing the criteria used by the Department of Defense in determining its need for generals and flag officers. The legislators sought the GAO portion of the inquiry because they wanted an outside agency to analyze the standards by which the Marines and other services justified the need for more generals or admirals.[109]

The 1997 congressional mandate for an inquiry into G/FOs was unusual in its charge fully to cover RC G/FOs along with officers in the AC. Pub.L.No. 104–201 required the secretary of defense to submit a report to Congress within six months, containing, among other things, any recommendations to revise limitations on G/FO grade authorizations and distribution, as well as recommendations regarding the "statutory designation of the positions and grades of any additional general and flag officers" in the reserve commands codified by the same Pub.L.No. 104–201.[110] Pub.L.No. 104–201, as noted, codified Army Reserve, Naval Reserve, Marine Corps Reserve, and Air Force Reserve Commands and established the chiefs of the services' reserve components as the commanders of those commands.[111] The secretary of defense was to include in the mandated report his views on whether to exempt reserve G/FOs from active-duty general/flag officer ceilings. He was also to state whether current provisions of law adequately recognize the significantly increased role of the reserve components in service-specific and joint operations and whether the provisions permit the assignment of G/FOs to AC and RC positions with pay grades commensurate with the scope of the positions' duties and responsibilities.

When the report mandated by the 1997 act was delayed, advocates for the reserve components proposed a command equity amendment to the National Defense Authorization Act

---

[107] West.

[108] "General Critiques Modern Military: Management Should be Cut, Not Combat Structure, He Warns," *The Virginian Pilot*, September 9, 1996, http://scholar.lib.vt.edu/VA-news/VA-Pilot/issues/1996/vp960909/0909 0029.htm.

[109] William L Hendrix, "Open and Candid Exchange Highlights Reserve and Guard Association Roundtable," *The Officer* 74, no. 3 (April 1998): 36–39.

[110] Hendrix, 37.

[111] Hendrix, 37.

for Fiscal Year 2000 that called for three-star ranks for the top reserve officers.[112] On October 5, 1999, Pub.L.No. 106–65, National Defense Authorization Act, FY 2000, section 554, "Grade of Chiefs of Reserve Components and additional General Officers at the National Guard Bureau," put into effect discretionary authority to promote the reserve chiefs and the National Guard directors to lieutenant general/vice admiral. As the act was passed, several senators warned DOD that if it did not act voluntarily to promote the officers, a law would be enacted in the following year requiring such promotions. The senators anticipated some reluctance on the part of the services, because they were expressly not given relief from senior grade and general and flag officer limits. Some in the services held that without such an exemption, they were not in a position to recommend promoting the RC leadership. When the services failed to exercise their discretionary authority, Congress indeed made the three-star rank mandatory with the enactment in October 2000 of Pub.L.No. 106–398, authorizing Department of Defense appropriations for fiscal year 2001, an act that also provided for a corresponding increase of O–9 authorizations.

Throughout the campaign to elevate the top reserve leadership to three stars, advocates for the reserves faced a challenging situation, since they had to make their case in the context of a major drawdown of the active component. The AC was in the process of reducing its overall officer corps to correspond with changes in force structure and missions. The Army and the Air Force, for instance, together lost about 100 generals between 1991 and 1999, and were left, respectively, with 36 and 35 three-star authorizations out of the DOD services' total of 109 three-star authorizations. In this context of scarcity, reserve advocates sought ways to circumvent direct competition with the active component for resources—i.e., O–9 authorizations—while still increasing the opportunities of the RC to be promoted above O–8. It was to avoid such competition that the Reserve Officers Association, for instance, consistently recommended that the reserve chiefs and other reserve G/FOs on active duty be excluded from statutory and administrative ceilings on active-duty G/FOs.[113] At the same time, the ROA and other reserve advocates did not relent in arguing that rank increases not only were warranted by the growing role of the reserves, but also were imperative for the optimal performance of the military. In particular, a prevalent argument for increased reserve officer representation above O–8 referred to the need for the reserves, in view of their ever-larger role in operations, to have, as reserve

---

[112] U.S. Congress, Senate, "Senate Floor Statement of Senator Sessions."
[113] "ROA Legislative Initiatives," 18.

advocate Senator Sessions said, "a stronger voice in decision-making and resource allocation within the Pentagon."[114] Whereas the most common argument for greater G/FO strength in the active components was that joint requirements were ever-increasing, the most common argument for greater numbers of senior reserve officers, particularly at the O–9 and O–10 levels, was the need for the reserve components to have greater institutional power. This argument about voice or greater institutional power, advanced in the recent testimony before the Commission on the National Guard and Reserves, has been put forward for a considerable number of years.[115] The increase in rank for the reserve chiefs and directors was considered important for effective reserve participation in policy-making processes within the Department of Defense and, particularly, in the budgetary competition for dwindling resources. Similar arguments have been advanced in the decade-long campaign, ultimately successful in 2007, to raise the rank of the chief of the National Guard Bureau (CNGB) from lieutenant general to general.[116] As Senator Kit Bond (R–Missouri) said in a March 8, 2006, congressional hearing on the rank of the CNGB,

> I've been around the military long enough to know that if you're in a room with a guy with more stars on his shoulder, he's the one that does the talking, and if you're lucky, you get to listen, not talk.[117]

The Quest for More Joint-Duty Opportunities

A related issue to the preoccupation with greater institutional power to be gained by higher grades was the issue of enhanced opportunities for reservists to gain joint experience and education. The Goldwater–Nichols Department of Defense Reorganization Act of 1986 requires officers to have served in a joint-duty position to advance above field-grade ranks. Thus, officers of various ranks, including one- and two-star generals, usually must serve in joint-duty positions at a given rank if they are to be considered for promotion. Reserve advocates have long voiced the concern that National Guard and reserve G/FOs lack sufficient opportunities for the joint

---

[114] U.S. Congress, Senate, "Senate Floor Statement of Senator Sessions."
[115] Stephen P. Anderson, Frank A. Edens, Claire J Gilstad, and Fred R. Becker, "ROA Testimony on Capitol Hill," *The Officer*, June 1, 1999, 20–26, http://www.proquest.com/ (accessed through Proquest, August 28, 2007).
[116] See Commission on the National Guard and Reserves, *Second Report to Congress*, March 1, 2007, http://www.cngr.gov.
[117] Commission on the National Guard and Reserves, Congressional Transcripts, Congressional Hearings, "Commission on the National Guard and Reserves Holds Hearing on National Guard and Reserve Operations and Roles," March 8, 2006, http://www.ngaus.org/ngaus/files/ccLibraryFiles/Filename/000000001265/Commission%20on%20Roles%20and%20Mission%203-8-06.pdf.

duty that is the sine qua non for serious consideration for O–9 and O–10 positions.[118] Advocates have long pressed to increase such opportunities in order to create a viable pool of reserve officers from which to choose more senior officers—officers above O–8 rank. Such advocates achieved several successes with the recent establishment in Title 10 of 11 joint-duty set-aside positions, the "Chairman's 10" in fiscal year 2000 and one additional position in 2006—positions discussed above. The formulation of the legislation on these set-aside positions amounted to a compromise that addressed primary concerns of both the active and reserve components. The major concern of the active components was not to lose G/FO authorizations to the reserve components. The reserve components' primary concern was to put policies in place that enhance the opportunities for reserve officers to gain joint qualifications for O–9 and O–10 positions. The result was a provision that gave no end-strength relief to the reserves, but enhanced the opportunity for reserve officers to gain the "significant joint-duty experience " that is a precondition for higher office. The Chairman's 10 allowed reserve officers to gain joint-duty experience without the individual counting against active-component end strength.

CONCLUSION

Recent modifications to Title 10, such as the Chairman's 10, bespeak congressional awareness of the concerns of reserve advocates with respect to the reserve G/FO corps. Reserve advocates have argued that the reserve G/FO corps has not been able to wield institutional power commensurate with the responsibilities of, and recent reliance upon, the reserves. In the interests of securing greater institutional power for the reserves, reserve advocates have pressed for, and succeeded in gaining, the promulgation in Title 10 of a number of changes that affect the G/FO corps. These changes include mainly the 11 recent joint-duty set-asides for reserve officers—the Chairman's 10, plus one—the designation of additional positions above O–8 for the RC's top leadership, and the creation of the reserve commands that will now have three-star generals as their heads. The changes in Title 10 have not included increases in the baseline number ceiling for reserve G/FOs. Reserve G/FO authorizations have seen neither increases nor decreases since they were first specified in national legislation, despite the fact that overall reserve numbers have

---

[118] Harry Thie and Margaret C. Harrell, et al, *Framing a Strategic Approach for Reserve Component Joint Officer Management*, MG–306–OSD, RAND National Defense Research Institute, 2006, http://www.rand.org/pubs/mono graphs/2006/RAND_MG517.sum.pdf.

fluctuated, with a downward trend through the 1990s, albeit a slighter declining trend than that affecting the AC. The downward trend in the overall size and officer strength of the RC did not prompt the same reduction in authorized G/FO strength that the AC saw. However, the charge of "officer-heaviness" periodically leveled against the AC has not appeared in discussions of the RC G/FO corps. To the contrary, the view has persisted that the RC has been shortchanged in its G/FO authorization compared to the AC.

APPENDIX 1: Three Decades of Force Strength Statistics

The statistics below are from the following source:

U.S. Department of Defense, Office of the Under Secretary of Defense (Personnel and Readiness), "2005 Population Representation in the Military Services," March 2007, https://humrro03.securesites.net/pop rep/poprep05/appendixd/d_21.html.

Table D–11. Active Component Enlisted Strength, FYs 1964, 1973–2005 (in Thousands)

FISCAL YEAR	SERVICE				TOTAL DOD
	ARMY	NAVY	MARINE CORPS	AIR FORCE	
1964	860.5	585.4	172.9	720.6	2329.4
1973	682.0	490.0	176.8	571.8	1921.0
1974	674.5	475.5	170.1	529.1	1849.0
1975	678.3	466.1	177.4	503.2	1825.0
1976	677.7	457.7	173.5	481.2	1790.1
1977	680.1	462.2	173.1	469.9	1785.2
1978	669.6	463.2	172.4	469.9	1775.0
1979	657.2	457.1	167.0	458.9	1740.3
1980	673.9	459.6	170.3	455.9	1759.7
1981	675.1	470.2	172.3	466.5	1784.0
1982	672.7	481.2	173.4	476.5	1803.8
1983	669.4	484.6	174.1	483.0	1811.1
1984	667.7	491.3	175.9	486.4	1821.3
1985	666.6	495.4	177.9	488.6	1828.5
1986	666.7	504.4	178.6	494.7	1844.3
1987	668.4	510.2	177.0	495.2	1853.3
1988	660.4	515.6	177.3	466.9	1820.1
1989	658.3	515.9	176.9	462.8	1813.9
1990	623.5	501.5	176.5	430.8	1732.4
1991	602.6	494.5	174.1	409.4	1680.5
1992	511.3	467.5	165.2	375.7	1519.8
1993	480.3	438.9	160.1	356.1	1435.4
1994	451.4	401.7	156.3	341.3	1350.7
1995	421.5	370.9	156.8	317.9	1267.2
1996	405.1	354.1	157.0	308.6	1224.9
1997	408.1	334.2	156.2	299.4	1197.9
1998	402.0	322.1	155.3	291.6	1170.9
1999	396.2	314.3	154.8	286.2	1151.4
2000	402.2	314.1	155.0	282.3	1153.6
2001	400.3	318.1	154.7	280.3	1153.4
2002	406.2	324.7	155.6	292.5	1179.0
2003	413.7	322.0	158.8	297.3	1191.8
2004	413.5	313.9	158.4	298.3	1184.1
2005	405.3	305.0	161.0	276.1	1147.4

Table D–17. Active Component Officer Strength, FYs 1973–2005

FISCAL YEAR	SERVICE				
	ARMY	NAVY	MARINE CORPS	AIR FORCE	TOTAL DOD
1973	101,194	66,337	17,784	114,962	300,277
1974	91,872	63,380	17,421	110,437	283,110
1975	87,215	60,422	17,080	102,849	267,566
1976	85,600	59,992	17,594	99,228	262,414
1977	84,627	60,274	17,524	96,244	258,669
1978	84,330	59,672	17,180	95,462	256,644
1979	84,496	59,189	16,934	96,129	256,748
1980	85,352	60,237	16,974	97,901	260,464
1981	87,923	62,678	17,091	99,630	267,322
1982	88,984	64,571	17,712	102,188	273,455
1983	91,084	66,874	18,583	104,879	281,420
1984	92,796	65,796	18,945	106,239	283,783
1985	94,372	67,521	18,697	108,400	288,990
1986	94,845	68,922	18,734	109,051	291,552
1987	93,160	69,071	18,730	107,340	288,301
1988	92,170	69,576	18,558	105,127	285,431
1989	91,900	69,475	18,466	103,699	283,540
1990	89,672	69,426	18,105	100,047	277,250
1991	88,747	67,980	17,775	96,600	271,102
1992	81,312	66,253	17,270	90,378	255,213
1993	75,062	63,608	16,547	84,076	239,293
1994	72,410	59,265	16,003	81,004	228,682
1995	70,814	56,408	15,852	78,444	221,518
1996	68,971	55,602	16,028	76,389	216,990
1997	67,994	54,382	16,002	73,984	212,362
1998	66,980	53,206	16,075	71,893	208,154
1999	66,104	52,136	16,055	70,321	204,616
2000	65,352	51,540	16,008	69,022	201,922
2001	64,797	51,928	16,160	68,038	200,923
2002	66,583	52,961	16,402	71,687	207,633
2003	67,953	53,323	16,787	73,643	211,706
2004	68,634	52,707	16,742	74,304	212,387
2005	68,932	51,291	16,879	73,251	210,353

Table D–20. Reserve Component Enlisted Strength, FYs 1974–2005

FISCAL YEAR	COMPONENT						TOTAL DOD
	ARNG	USAR	USNR	USMCR	ANG	USAFR	
1974	356,374	193,855	94,048	29,069	82,017	35,309	790,672
1975	356,286	183,866	81,157	28,615	82,162	39,235	771,321
1976	332,696	156,221	78,670	26,952	79,865	36,945	711,349
1977	320,733	153,736	72,281	28,371	80,621	38,211	693,953
1978	306,690	149,890	65,166	30,134	80,517	41,158	673,555
1979	309,679	154,408	71,070	30,800	81,876	43,768	691,601
1980	329,298	169,165	70,010	33,002	84,382	45,954	731,811
1981	350,645	188,103	72,608	34,559	85,915	52,686	784,516
1982	367,214	208,617	75,674	37,104	88,140	50,553	827,302
1983	375,500	216,218	88,474	39,005	89,500	52,810	861,507
1984	392,412	222,188	98,187	37,444	92,178	55,340	897,749
1985	397,612	238,220	106,529	38,204	96,361	59,599	936,525
1986	402,628	253,070	116,640	38,123	99,231	62,505	972,197
1987	406,487	255,291	121,938	38,721	100,827	63,855	987,119
1988	406,966	253,467	121,653	39,930	101,261	65,567	988,844
1989	406,848	256,872	122,537	39,948	101,980	66,126	994,311
1990	394,060	248,326	123,117	40,903	103,637	66,566	976,609
1991	395,988	249,626	123,727	41,472	103,670	67,603	982,086
1992	378,904	245,135	115,341	38,748	104,758	65,806	948,692
1993	363,263	219,610	105,254	38,092	102,920	64,720	893,859
1994	351,390	206,849	86,300	36,860	99,711	63,411	844,521
1995	331,559	191,558	79,827	36,292	96,305	62,144	797,685
1996	328,141	179,967	77,376	37,256	97,153	57,615	777,508
1997	329,288	168,596	75,373	37,254	96,713	56,068	763,295
1998	323,150	161,286	73,490	36,620	94,861	56,032	745,439
1999	319,161	161,930	69,999	35,947	92,424	55,557	735,018
2000	315,645	165,053	67,999	35,699	93,019	55,676	733,091
2001	315,250	164,760	68,872	35,881	95,060	56,819	736,642
2002	314,629	166,258	69,692	36,144	98,141	59,330	744,194
2003	314,246	171,593	69,370	37,386	94,435	57,949	744,979
2004	306,234	165,781	64,359	36,178	93,188	58,598	724,338
2005	296,623	152,070	59,471	36,539	92,758	59,126	696,587

Table D–21. Reserve Component Officer* Strength, FYs 1974-2005

FISCAL YEAR	COMPONENT						TOTAL DOD
	ARNG	USAR	USNR	USMCR	ANG	USAFR	
1974	28,260	34,566	17,350	2,294	11,527	11,703	105,700
1975	27,502	34,308	17,181	2,196	11,379	11,576	104,142
1976	27,472	32,372	18,030	2,038	11,225	12,108	103,245
1977	27,079	32,152	17,207	2,242	11,130	12,174	101,984
1978	27,287	32,222	16,851	2,208	11,084	12,722	102,374
1979	28,468	32,034	16,520	2,123	11,447	12,889	103,481
1980	29,616	32,861	16,050	2,001	11,832	12,963	105,323
1981	30,396	34,030	16,247	2,104	12,348	13,054	108,179
1982	32,094	43,902	17,413	2,427	12,500	13,887	122,223
1983	32,892	45,685	19,993	2,493	12,657	14,415	128,135
1984	32,856	48,362	21,750	2,647	12,824	14,976	133,415
1985	33,163	49,195	22,737	2,846	13,029	15,614	136,584
1986	34,164	51,834	24,356	2,922	13,357	16,013	142,646
1987	35,748	53,554	25,646	3,023	13,766	16,559	148,296
1988	38,293	54,553	27,326	3,138	13,959	16,548	153,817
1989	40,233	57,491	28,532	3,144	14,080	17,087	160,567
1990	40,545	57,011	29,275	3,130	14,149	17,246	161,356
1991	40,732	55,460	27,387	2,971	14,116	16,935	157,601
1992	38,642	53,217	26,609	2,989	14,325	16,067	151,849
1993	37,600	51,829	26,775	3,142	14,242	15,842	149,430
1994	36,686	48,800	21,021	3,352	13,876	16,210	139,945
1995	34,932	45,789	20,470	4,150	13,520	16,123	134,984
1996	33,504	42,999	20,283	4,299	13,331	16,053	130,469
1997	32,585	41,304	19,664	4,232	13,306	15,918	127,009
1998	31,306	40,665	19,405	3,760	13,235	15,938	124,309
1999	30,418	41,933	18,907	3,565	13,291	16,215	124,329
2000	29,664	38,956	18,691	3,544	13,346	16,664	120,865
2001	29,002	38,118	18,808	3,512	13,425	16,938	119,803
2002	29,023	37,710	18,060	3,370	13,930	17,302	119,395
2003	29,572	37,615	18,596	3,282	13,702	16,805	119,572
2004	29,806	35,828	18,014	3,097	13,634	16,724	117,103
2005	29,952	34,406	16,824	3,030	13,672	16,676	114,560

* Excluding warrant officers

Source: Based on U.S. Department of Defense, Office of the Under Secretary of Defense (Personnel and Readiness), "2005 Population Representation in the Military Services," March 2007, https://humrro03.securesites.net/poprep/poprep05/appendixd/d_21.html.

APPENDIX 2: Reserve Component Categories

All members of a service's reserve component are assigned to one of three reserve categories: Ready Reserve, Standby Reserve, and Retired Reserve. The first of these categories, by far the largest, comprises three subcategories, the Selected Reserve, the Individual Ready Reserve, and the Inactive National Guard, and these subcategories in turn have further subcategories, as described in the following source:

> U.S. Department of Defense, Office of the Assistant Secretary of Defense (Reserve Affairs), *Reserve Component Categories of the Reserve Components of the Armed Forces* (Rev. September 2005), http://www.defenselink.mil/ra/ documents/RC101%20Handbook-updated%2020%20Sep%2005.pdf.

This DOD source describes each of the categories of reservists, as follows:

- The **Ready Reserve** comprises military members of the Reserve and National Guard, organized in units or as individuals, liable for recall to active duty to augment the active components in time of war or national emergency. The Ready Reserve consists of three reserve component subcategories:
  - The **Selected Reserve** consists of those units and individuals within the Ready Reserve designated by their respective Services as so essential to initial wartime missions that they have priority over all other Reserves. The Selected Reserve consists of additional subcategories:
    - **Drilling Reservists in Units** are trained unit members who participate in unit training activities on a part-time basis.
    - **Training Pipeline (non-deployable account)** personnel are enlisted members of the Selected Reserve who have not yet completed initial active duty for training (IADT) and officers who are in training for professional categories or in undergraduate flying training.
    - **Individual Mobilization Augmentees (IMAs)** are trained individuals assigned to an active component, Selective Service System, or Federal Emergency Management Agency (FEMA) organization's billet which must be filled on or shortly after mobilization. IMAs participate in training activities on a part-time basis with an active component unit in preparation for recall in a mobilization.
    - **Active Guard/Reserve (AGR)** are National Guard or Reserve members of the Selected Reserve who are ordered to active-duty or full-time National Guard duty for the purpose of organizing, administering, recruiting, instructing, or training the reserve component units.
  - **Individual Ready Reserve (IRR)** personnel provide a manpower pool comprised principally of individuals who have had training, have previously served in an active duty component or in the Selected Reserve, and have some period of their military service obligation remaining.
  - **Inactive National Guard (ING)** personnel provide a manpower pool comprised principally of individuals who have had training and have served in an active duty

component or in the Selected Reserve, and who have some period of their service obligation remaining.

- The **Standby Reserve** consists of personnel who maintain their affiliation without being in the Ready Reserve, who have been designated key civilian employees, or who have a temporary hardship. They are not required to perform training and are not part of units but create a pool of trained individuals who could be mobilized to fill manpower needs in specific skills.
    - o **Active Status List** are those Standby Reservists temporarily assigned for hardship or other cogent reason; those not having fulfilled their military service obligation or those retained in active status when provided for by law; or those members of Congress and others identified by their employers as "key personnel" and who have been removed from the Ready Reserve because they are critical to the national security in their civilian employment.
    - o **Inactive Status List** are those Standby Reservists who are not required by law or regulation to remain in an active program and who retain their Reserve affiliation in a nonparticipating status, and those who have skills which may be of possible future use to the Armed Force concerned.
- The **Retired Reserve** consists of all Reserve officers and enlisted personnel who receive retired pay on the basis of active duty and/or reserve service; all Reserve officers and enlisted personnel who are otherwise eligible for retired pay but have not reached age 60, who have not elected discharge and are not voluntary members of the Ready or Standby Reserve; and other retired reservists under certain conditions.

BIBLIOGRAPHY

Anderson, Stephen P., Frank A. Edens, Claire J. Gilstad, and Fred R. Becker. "ROA Testimony on Capitol Hill." *The Officer*, June 1, 1999, 20–26. http://www.proquest.com/ (accessed through Proquest August 28, 2007).

Asch, Beth J. *Reserve Supply in the Post-Desert Storm Recruiting Environment*. Santa Monica: Rand, 1993. http://www.rand.org/pubs/monograph_reports/2006/MR224.pdf.

Baird , Major Stephen W. "Too Many General Officers?" 1991. http://www.globalsecurity. org/military/library/report/1991/BSW.htm.

Cathcart, Sue, and Christopher Prawdzik. "ROPMA: Challenged, Some Officers Excel Under New Rules." *National Guard* 56, no. 6 (July 2002): 28–30.

Cohen, William. "Report of the Chairman of the Reserve Forces Policy Board," in *Annual Report to the President and the Congress*. 2000. http://www.dod.mil/execsec/adr2000/index.html.

Commission on the National Guard and Reserves. *Hearing on Proposed Changes to the National Guard*. January 31, 2007 (testimony of General Peter Pace). http://www.cngr.gov/hearing 13107/0131cngr-3.pdf.

Commission on the National Guard and Reserves. *Second Report to Congress*. March 1, 2007. http://www.cngr.gov.

Edens, Colonel Frank. "The Chronology of Obtaining a Three-Star CAR and Establishing an Army Reserve Command." *Washington Update: Senior Army Reserve Commanders Association* 20, no. 2 (July 2001): 6. http://sarca.us/News/update-0107.pdf.

"General Critiques Modern Military: Management Should be Cut, Not Combat Structure, He Warns." *The Virginian Pilot*, September 9, 1996. http://scholar.lib.vt.edu/VA-news/VA-Pilot/issues/1996/vp960909/09090029.htm.

Hendrix, William L. "Open and Candid Exchange Highlights Reserve and Guard Association Roundtable." *The Officer* 74, no. 3 (April 1998): 36–39.

Maze, Rick. "Senate Balks at Proposal for 363 More Flag Officers." *Air Force Times*, August 22, 1988.

Maze, Rick. "Senate Panel Favors 20% Fewer Top Officers." *Air Force Times*, July 30, 1990.

McCalla, Mary Ellen, et al. *Description of Officers and Enlisted Personnel in the U.S. Selected Reserve: 1986. A Report Based on the 1986 Reserve Components Survey*. U. S. Department of Defense, Defense Manpower Data Center, n.d.

Nestler, Major Scott T. "Officer Bloat or Changing Requirements?" *Army Magazine*, February 1, 2004. http://www.ausa.org/webpub/DeptArmyMagazine.nsf/byid/CCRN-6CCSBW.

Reserve Officers Association. "ROA Legislative Initiatives." *The Officer*, May 2007. http://www.roa.org/site/DocServer/0705_officer.pdf?docID=1961.

"Sayen Report: Officer Bloat Creates the Shortage of Captains." July 16, 2000. http://www.d-n-i.net/fcs/comments/c372.htm#Reference%201.

Thie, Harry J., et al. *Future Career Management Systems for U.S. Military Officers*. MR470, RAND Arroyo Center, 1994. http://www.rand.org/pubs/monograph_reports/MR470/mr470.ch2.pdf.

Thie, Harry J., and Jefferson P. Marquis. *The Present Military Personnel Management Framework: Where It Came From*. PM–1247–OSD, September 2001. http://www.defenselink.mil/prhome/docs/military_hr_stratplan3.pdf.

Thie, Harry, and Margaret C. Harrell, et al. *Framing a Strategic Approach for Reserve Component Joint Officer Management*. MG–306–OSD, RAND National Defense Research Institute, 2006. http://www.rand.org/pubs/monographs/2006/RAND_MG517.sum.pdf.

U.S. Army. Center of Military History. *Army Historical Summary: FY 1994*. http://www.army.mil/cmhpg/books/DAHSUM/1994/ch09.htm.

U.S. Army. Center of Military History. *Army Historical Summary: FY 1996*. http://www.army.mil/cmhpg/books/DAHSUM/1996/ch01.htm.

U.S. Army. Center of Military History. "Manning the Army." Chapter 5 in *Army Historical Summary: Fiscal Year 1980*. http://www.army.mil/CMH/books/DAHSUM/1980/ch05.htm.

U.S. Army. Center of Military History. "Reserve Components." Chapter 8 in *Army Historical Summary: Fiscal Year 1989*. http://www.army.mil/cmh-pg/books/DAHSUM/1989/CH8.htm.

U.S. Army. Center of Military History. "Staffing the Army." Chapter 2 in *Army Historical Summary: Fiscal Year 1985*. http://www.army.mil/CMH/books/DAHSUM/1985/ch02.htm.

U.S. Army. Center of Military History. "Structuring the Force: The Army and Total Force Policy." Chapter 8 in *Army Historical Summary: Fiscal Years 1990 and 1991*. http://www.army. mil/cmh/books/DAHSUM/1990-91/ch08.htm.

U.S. Census Bureau. *Statistical Abstract of the United States: 2007*. http://www.census.gov/prod/2006pubs/07statab/defense.pdf.

U.S. Congress. House of Representatives. Committee on National Security. Subcommittee on Military Personnel. *Hearings on National Defense Authorization Act for FY 1998: H.R. 1119 and Oversight of Previously Authorized Programs.* 105th Cong., 1st sess., April 8, 1997. http://commdocs.house.gov/committees/security/has058020.000/has058020_2. HTM.

U.S. Congress. Senate. "Senate Floor Statement of Senator Sessions: Sessions Amendment No. 465 Offered To S. 1059, National Defense Authorization Act for Fiscal Year 2000." May 27, 1999. http://sessions.senate.gov/pressapp/record.cfm?id=178423.

U.S. Congress. Senate. Committee on Armed Services. Subcommittee on Manpower and Personnel. *General and Flag Officer Requirements.* 100th Cong., 2d sess., August 10, 1988 (Statement of Grant Green, Jr., Assistant Secretary of Defense for Force Management and Personnel).

U.S. Congressional Budget Office. "CBO Paper: The Drawdown of the Military Officer Corps." November 1999. http://www.cbo.gov/ftpdocs/17xx/doc1772/drawdown.pdf.

U. S. Department of Defense. *Defense Officer Requirements Study.* March 1988, 32–36.

U. S. Department of Defense. *DOD Instruction, Number 1332.32.* December 27, 2006. http://www.dtic.mil/whs/directives/corres/pdf/133232p.pdf.

U.S. Department of Defense. "Reserve Component Employment Study 2005 – Annex G/FO: Resourcing Panel Report." August 2, 1999. http://www.dod.mil/pubs/rces2005_ 0799g.html.

U. S. Department of Defense. Chairman of the Joint Chiefs of Staff. "Manpower and Personnel Actions Involving General and Flag Officers." *Chairman of the Joint Chiefs of Staff Instruction (CJCSI) 1331.01C.* July 22, 2005, current as of July 31, 2006. http://www.dtic.mil/cjcs_directives/cdata/ unlimit/1331_01.pdf.

U.S. Department of Defense. Defense Manpower Data Center. Statistical Information Analysis Division. *Selected Manpower Statistics*, Table 5–15: Department of Defense, Total Distribution of the Individual Ready Reserve/Inactive National Guard by Grade. September 30, 2005. http://siadapp.dmdc.osd.mil/personnel/M01/fy05/m01fy05.pdf.

U.S. Department of Defense. Office of the Assistant Secretary of Defense (Public Affairs). "National Guard, Reserve—Central Parts of Total Force: Prepared Statement of Deborah R. Lee, Assistant Secretary of Defense for Reserve Affairs." Testimony before the Readiness Subcommittee, Senate Armed Services Committee, February 6, 1996. http://www.defenselink.mil/speeches/speech.aspx?speechid=874.

U.S. Department of Defense. Office of the Assistant Secretary of Defense (Reserve Affairs). *Reserve Component Categories of the Reserve Components of the Armed Forces* (Rev.

September 2005). http://www.defenselink.mil/ra/documents/RC101%20Handbook-updated%2020%20Sep%2005.pdf.

U.S. Department of Defense. Office of the Under Secretary of Defense (Personnel and Readiness). *Review of Active Duty and Reserve General and Flag Officer Authorizations.* Washington, DC, March 2003.

U.S. General Accounting Office (GAO). *General And Flag Officers: DOD's Study Needs Adjustments: Testimony Before the Subcommittee on Military Personnel, Committee on National Security, House of Representatives* (statement of Mark E. Gebicke, Director, Military Operations and Capabilities Issues, National Security and International Affairs Division). GAO/T–NSIAD–97–122, April 8, 1997. http://www.gao.gov/archive/1997/ns97122t.pdf.

U.S. General Accounting Office (GAO). *General And Flag Officers: Number Required Is Unclear Based On DOD's Draft Report.* GAO/NSIAD–97–160. Washington, DC, June 1997. http://www.gao.gov/archive/1997/ns97160.pdf.

U.S. General Accounting Office (GAO). *Military Personnel: High Aggregate Personnel Levels Maintained Throughout Drawdown.* GAO/NSIAD–95–97. Washington, DC, June 1995. http://archive.gao.gov/t2pbat1/154251.pdf.

U.S. Government Accountability Office (GAO). "Appendix I: Sixteen Factors Used to Validate General and Flag Officer Requirements," *Military Personnel: General and Flag Officer Requirements Are Unclear Based on DOD's 2003 Report to Congress.* GAO–04–488. Washington, DC, April 2004, http://www.gao.gov/cgi-bin/getrpt?GAO-04-488.

U.S. Government Accountability Office (GAO). *Military Personnel: A Strategic Approach Is Needed to Address Long-Term Guard and Reserve Force Availability.* GAO–05–285T. Washington, DC, February 2, 2005.

U.S. Government Accountability Office (GAO). *Military Personnel: DOD Could Make Greater Use of Existing Legislative Authority to Manage General and Flag Officer Careers.* GAO–04–1003. Washington, DC, September 2004. http://www.gao.gov/cgi-bin/getrpt? GAO-04-1003.

U.S. Government Accountability Office (GAO). *Military Personnel: DOD Needs to Address Long-Term Reserve Force Availability and Related Mobilization and Demobilization Issues.* GAO–04–1031. Washington, DC, September 15, 2004.

U.S. Government Accountability Office (GAO). *Military Personnel: General and Flag Officer Requirements Are Unclear Based on DOD's 2003 Report to Congress.* GAO–04–488. Washington, DC, April 2004. http://www.gao.gov/cgi-bin/getrpt?GAO-04-488.

U.S. Government Accountability Office (GAO). *Military Personnel: Reserve Components Need Guidance to Accurately and Consistently Account for Volunteers on Active Duty for*

Operational Support. GAO–07–93. Washington, DC, October 2006. http://www.gao.gov/new.items/d0793.pdf.

U.S. Government Accountability Office (GAO). *Reserve Forces: Actions Needed to Better Prepare the National Guard for Future Overseas and Domestic Missions*. GAO–05–21. Washington, DC, November 10, 2004.

U.S. Government Accountability Office (GAO). *Reserve Forces: Army National Guard's Role, Organization, and Equipment Need to Be Reexamined*. GAO–06–170T. Washington, DC, October 20, 2005.

West, Woody. "Old Story, New Title; No Time for Generals – Questionable Need for More Marine Generals and Navy Admirals." *Insight on the News*, November 4, 1996. http://findarticles.com/p/articles/mi_m1571/is_n41_v12/ai_18822628.

Zapanta, Albert C. "Transforming Reserve Forces," *Joint Force Quarterly*, December 2004.

Also used in the preparation of this report were Title 10, the U.S. Code, and various sources of U.S. Department of Defense statistics. The report relies on online versions of the U.S Code, particularly on the Web site of the Cornell University Law School: http://www.law.cornell.edu/uscode/#TITLES. For the military data used in the report, the author consulted statistical Web sites, including the Web site of the Defense Manpower Data Center, "DOD Personnel and Procurement Statistics, Personnel & Procurement Reports and Data Files." Also consulted were online versions of U.S. Department of Defense, Office of the Under Secretary of Defense for Personnel and Readiness, *Population Representation in the Military Services*, available through http://www.dod.mil/prhome/index.html, and the Web site of the Human Resources Research Organization (HumRRO): https://humrro03.securesites.net/poprep/poprep05/appendixd/d_21.html. These reports, which provide longitudinal data in Appendix D, have been available annually since 1974, when the Senate Committee on Armed Services, in Report 93–884, May 1974, mandated that the Department of Defense provide them.